I0759399

The Way Love Goes

THE WAY *Love* GOES

A Guide to Building a "Beaurtiful" and Everlasting Relationship

Da Brat & Judy

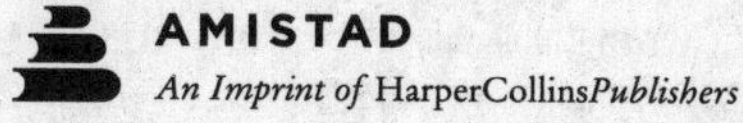

AMISTAD
An Imprint of HarperCollins*Publishers*

 For information, address HarperCollins Publishers, 195 Broadway, New York, NY 10007. In Europe, HarperCollins Publishers, Macken House, 39/40 Mayor Street Upper, Dublin 1, D01 C9W8, Ireland.

HarperCollins books may be purchased for educational, business, or sales promotional use. For information, please email the Special Markets Department at SPsales@harpercollins.com.

harpercollins.com

FIRST EDITION

Designed by Kyle O'Brien
Emoji art © Cali6ro/Shutterstock

Library of Congress Cataloging-in-Publication Data

Names: Da Brat (Musician), author. | Judy (Entrepreneur), author.
Title: The way love goes : a guide to building a "beaurtiful" and everlasting relationship / Da Brat and Judy.
Description: First edition. | New York : Amistad, HarperCollins, 2026. |
Identifiers: LCCN 2025002520 (print) | LCCN 2025002521 (ebook) |
ISBN 9780063349643 (hardcover) | ISBN 9780063349667 (ebook)
Subjects: LCSH: Da Brat (Musician) | Judy (Entrepreneur) | Rap musicians—United States—Biography. | Musicians' spouses—United States—Biography. | Relationship quality. | Communication in marriage. | Conduct of life. | LCGFT: Autobiographies.
Classification: LCC ML420.D103 A3 2025 (print) | LCC ML420.D103 (ebook) |
DDC 782.421649092/2 [B]—dc23/eng/20250124
LC record available at https://lccn.loc.gov/2025002520
LC ebook record available at https://lccn.loc.gov/2025002521

---

25 26 27 28 29 LBC 5 4 3 2 1

To our *beaurtiful* family, parents, grandparents, children, and our entire village that keep our dreams and aspirations vivid. . . . We love and appreciate you. And last but not least, our loyal fans and followers who never doubted and still believe in our unconditional love for one another. . . . Thank you.

"Beaurtiful," I just want you to know

You're my favorite girl!

—**Snoop Dogg, "Beautiful"**

Table of Contents

Introduction

Let's face it. Love is quite the motherfucker. Yes, that's a harsh way to describe it, but we're adults so there's no need to mince words. Plus, it's true. It's unfortunate that this remarkable (and it really is when you find it), soul-stirring emotion that the bible claims is patient and kind, doesn't envy or boast, and isn't proud doesn't play by any rules. It does what it wants when it wants. It damn sure doesn't come when you need it and most definitely doesn't come when you want it.

If you're a single Black woman, you've undoubtedly heard that your outlook for finding love is pretty bleak. We won't bother getting into the "reasons." That's not what this book is about. We'll leave that discussion to the relationship experts, podcast bros, and social media "know-it-alls" to argue back and forth about why, when compared to other groups, love's navigational system seems to be broken for us. It's a point of view that's endlessly shared across all forms of media. Every day, folks are finding new ways to tell sistas that they can put the word out by bat signal that they're looking for "the one," sign up for every dating app, or spend hours working on a vision board to "manifest" their ideal partner, but it's not going to do any good. Apparently, love's

GPS has trouble finding our locations so don't bother leaving the porch light on. Is it a wonder why so many Black women are discouraged and have given up on love?

You don't have to be a Black woman—or a woman at all—to know that even for the most positive and hopeful individual, love is still hard to find. Sure, there are those who say it's not hard at all and it's not love's GPS that's broken, but our pickers. Again, we'll leave that discussion to others.

When it comes to love, what all sides of the debate **can** agree on is that it's totally **unpredictable**. The moment it shows up in your life, it's so damn bold that it will knock you on your ass as if to say, "gotcha, bitch!" If that ain't a motherfucker, we don't know what is. You do eventually recover from love's powerful one-two punch, but not without it leaving you dazed and confused and asking, *What the fuck just happened?* And just when you think you're good and in control, you realize two of your most important organs—your heart and mind—no longer apparently belong to you. You're not quite sure when someone else got in the driver's seat, but now your every waking thought seems to be about a certain someone whom you send daily "hey big head" text messages to, call to talk about the aspects of your day, and snuggle up to for regular Tubi-and-chill sessions.

Yep. That's this thing called love. And how do we know? Unless you've been living under a rock, it happened to us! Honestly, neither one of us had this love story on our bingo cards. Who knew that this amazing, heart-stopping experience would come in a package that includes a bomb-ass friendship, a platinum-selling rap star, a self-made millionaire, two pretty faces, and one big ole booty? But it did. And that describes who we are in a nutshell—Da Brat and Jesseca, aka DaRealBBJudy—two Black women who are famous, rich, lesbian, married, and, most important, madly in love with each other and the life we are building together. It's been more than seven years that we have been a couple, and the biggest lesson we've learned thus far is that this thing called love is powerful, inexplicable, and, at times, maddening, but it's also, as we like to say, the most *beaurtiful* feeling in the world. Let the church say, "Amen!"

Our journey to become this fabulous, married, same-sex couple began like most Hollywood love stories—with a meet-cute. Except, ours wasn't *that* cute. It was on a random day in Atlanta, Georgia. We were brought together through a business opportunity. Our meeting was an awkward exchange that included a spilled drink, a dropped blunt (that ended up burning a hole through an expensive couch), and one of us stammering through her words.

Da Brat: Here's how it went down. . . . Judy had been traveling around the country speaking to aspiring entrepreneurs. Although she had previously hired me to do promotional work for her company, we had never met. When I learned she was going to be in Atlanta, I had to stop by to say *wassup* to possibly secure another opportunity to do more promo videos for her company. I also wanted to see in person this larger-than-life woman who always had something positive and inspirational to share with her millions of social media followers. In fact, it was one of her video messages that made me a fan of hers as well. I was going through a stressful time, and I stumbled across one of her posts while scrolling Instagram. And there she was—this pretty lady with big, beautiful gray hair sharing an uplifting message that touched my heart. The way she spoke made me feel that everything I was going through at that time was going to be okay. I immediately gave her a follow so I wouldn't miss any more of her uplifting messages.

But back to the story. . . . When I got to the location of Judy's speaking engagement, I was floored. The place was packed from the windows to the walls! I knew she was popular, but I wasn't expecting to see that kind of turnout. Judy's assistant said she would let Judy know I was in the house so she and I could officially meet. But there were so many people vying for Judy's attention that it took her about thirty minutes to get to me. Of course my celebrity ego pulled up. In my head I was thinking, *How is she gonna make me wait? I'm Da Brat!*

Judy finally made her way through the crowd to say hello to me. I thought she was just as beautiful as she appeared in her videos. We hugged and tried to make small talk, but it was just so loud and noisy in the room that it was hard to hold a conversation. I gave Judy my cell phone number and said we should link up later. She reached out after her event ended, and I invited her to visit me at the So So Def Recordings studio.

Judy's car pulled up and when she got out I was once again impressed! She was so cute in her outfit. She looked great at her seminar, but she changed her clothes for her visit to the studio. Her face was also beat to the gods. Her hair was poppin'. . . . Everything, better yet, SHE was on point. But she was dressed way too cute to be out and about in Atlanta all by herself. This woman didn't know where she had been invited to. The studio could have been in a bad location in a hood somewhere, and she showed up looking completely glamorous with her flashy jewelry and ten-inch fingernails. I was surprised she didn't have an entourage with her. There was no assistant, videographer, makeup artist. I thought for sure she would come with her team members, and we would knock out some more promo videos. Obviously, "work" was not on the agenda.

I took Judy on a tour of the recording studio. We chatted as I showed her some of my plaques and other achievements. I asked her about herself and the things she was interested in outside of her business. I was not prepared for her answer. Judy flat out said, "I'm interested in you." Huh? She had me totally fucked up. For the first time ever (yes, ever), I didn't know what to do or say. Try as I might, I couldn't keep my cool because all of a sudden I was feeling a serious case of butterflies. This attractive, self-made millionaire and owner of a small company that was making huge strides was interested in *me* of all people? GTFOH!

I was trying hard to play it off, but I couldn't keep it together. I was so nervous. I opted to do some cool shit to get my bearings. I lit a blunt but dropped the damn thing, and it burned a hole through an expensive studio couch. I poured myself a little Hennessy, but when I brought the cup up for a sip, I totally missed my mouth and spilled the drink on my shirt. Everything was going wrong. Like, the dumbest shit you could think of that the coolest motherfucker (which I thought I was) would not ever do was happening. I'm rarely caught off guard, but Judy's directness threw me for a loop. I didn't even know she was into women. It was also a big surprise that as a successful businesswoman, she would have an interest in a rapper. A platinum-selling superstar, but a rapper nonetheless!

DaRealBBJudy: I'll be honest. I went to the studio by myself because my *Beaurtiful*, a nickname I have given to Brat, said, "Let's link later." And well, that sounded like a date to me! So I showed up accordingly. Also, I am a big believer that everything happens for a reason. I was in Atlanta to speak to aspiring entrepreneurs about how I leveraged social media and my following to grow Kaleidoscope, my hair-products company. It was through my business that I was able to hire Brat, who's undeniably hip-hop royalty, to do promotional videos for my most popular product. But that endeavor was done through booking agents and managers. As she shared, we had never been in the same room before. So I know it wasn't a coincidence that she decided to come by my speaking engagement. It was fate. We were supposed to be in the same place at the same time. We were supposed to meet.

Beaurtiful thought her invitation to "link later" would be so I could talk to her about doing business. But she's right about one thing. I didn't have that in mind at all. I accepted an invitation to hang out because the woman is gorgeous! Not only is she attractive as hell, but she's very different from her rap persona. She's warm, incredibly inviting, and totally irresistible. So, yes, I wanted to spend some time together and get to know her better.

I hadn't been at the recording studio for more than ten or

fifteen minutes before I decided to make a move. I might have been a little overzealous by shooting my shot so quickly, but fearlessness is one of my character traits. I'm not totally fearless about everything, but when it comes to pursuing the things I want, I have no problem going after them. Plus, she asked me what I was interested in. I simply answered the question. I was interested in HER.

Beaurtiful's response was unforgettable. Who would have thought that this world-renowned, gangster rapper would come completely undone by me telling her I was interested in her? To be clear, she didn't just come undone, she totally lost her shit. I remained cool as I watched her try unsuccessfully to steer her way through her very first experience with "the butterflies." I wasn't as beside myself as she was, but I had some gut feelings of my own that something wonderful was happening between us.

For us, falling in love has been an organic experience. Since the moment our paths aligned and were affirmed by a strong physical attraction and deep personal connection, we have been having the time of our lives. We feel extremely blessed to find and experience this kind of love. But the road hasn't been without a few bumps. Like in most relationships, once the butterflies subsided and the newness of the relationship wore off, we had to face the reality that the person we had fallen head over heels in love with was imperfect. There isn't a couple anywhere on this big ole spinning rock called planet Earth who hasn't had to confront this realization while simultaneously trying not to start yet another argument about their beloved's annoying daily shortcomings. Everybody's got bothersome habits, but there's something extra irritating to the soul when the person you love never puts the toilet seat down, leaves squirts of toothpaste in the bathroom sink, drops their dirty drawers in the middle of the floor, spends too much money on shit y'all don't need, or, worse, takes a swig out of the carton and puts it back in the refrigerator. You're lucky to find someone who is your perfect match but somehow also irks the shit out of you? How Sway?

When it comes to relationships, there's an endless list of things we end up learning about our significant others that show up *after* the honeymoon phase. The question then becomes: In this unpredictable, brazen, *beaurtiful* thing called love, how do you keep the integrity of the bond strong and the relationship healthy when there are things about them that kinda sorta (correction: totally) get on your nerves?

As two high-profile Black women who defied the odds and found genuine love, we are often asked by our social media followers and fans of our TV show, *Brat Loves Judy*: How do we make it work? Courting and dating is one thing. Making a choice every single day to cultivate a lifelong, lasting bond is completely different.

So what's in our secret sauce? Well, that's what this book is about! Basically, we **adhere** to some rules, make **adjustments** when needed, and **assert** ourselves when something comes up so we don't sit and stew in anger and resentment. There's much more to maintaining a healthy relationship than that and to us specifically, but you'll have to keep reading. Our goal with this book is to take you on the journey with us as we share stories about our relationship that haven't been captured on our reality show. We are pulling the curtain all the way back to reveal how we have maneuvered through the good stuff—not just the high points but also the times we've been angry or disappointed with each other or ourselves. These situations have taught us some valuable lessons called "The Golden Rules," which have become an integral part of us being able to maintain a healthy, loving relationship.

Now it's time to address the elephant in the room. We know what you're thinking. Brat and Judy are lesbians so this must be a book for women who love women. Not necessarily. After reading how we love each other, you may be open to taking a dip in the lady pond. Or you may not. That's perfectly fine. To us, this thing called love is universal. The rules we live by can be applied to any relationship. By the way, we hate labels. So this is not a gay handbook for love. This is the story of two human beings who happen to be lesbians in love, who have learned how to make their marriage work. Our intention is to show that gay and lesbian couples are no different than hetero couples. We aren't unicorns. The unicorn is LOVE.

Last, when deciding to write this book, we discovered so much of who we are and how we show up in our relationship has to do with our life stories before we became a couple. We couldn't possibly write about this thing called love without also delving into some of our backstories that have undeniably shaped who we have become. Without these experiences neither of us would have been able to recognize love when it showed up in our lives, be inspired by it, and work hard to sustain it.

We're calling these short bites about us "reflections." You'll find them scattered throughout. Not only will they tell you a lot about who we are, but they'll also give you some insight into why we were so drawn to each other and determined to succeed at this thing called love.

Reflection

Da Brat

I met my first girlfriend when I was working on my album *Funkdafied*. I had flown to New York City from Atlanta to visit the offices of my record label, Columbia Records. There was this girl who worked there who I thought was supercool. She was a tomboy like me, and we shared a lot of similar interests. Before I left Columbia's office we exchanged numbers. We talked on the phone all the time. We would have marathon conversations, and neither of us would want to hang up. We'd often fall asleep on the phone. After several months I found myself wanting to hear her voice all the time. When I wasn't on the phone with her, I was thinking about calling her. I remember telling her, during one of our extended phone conversations, how I never wanted to get off the phone with her and when we did hang up that I missed her. I guess you can say that in my teenaged way, I confessed to having feelings for her. Apparently, she had feelings for me, too, because she said she felt the same way as I did.

Having grown up in a religious home, I was so unsure about how I felt. I even told her that I didn't think it was supposed to be happening this way. Despite my uncertainty she and I continued to talk to each other for long periods of time. We would spend time with each other when I would fly to New York for meetings at the record label. We eventually made plans for her to visit me in Atlanta. The first time she came to visit was when I had my first kiss with a girl.

Though I was falling hard for her, I still tried to hide my feelings from everyone else. It became even more difficult after she and I were intimate. I had never experienced anything like that before. It was more affection, compassion, and attention than I'd ever felt with a guy.

1 Communication

In retrospect, the way things transpired during our not-so-cute meet-cute/"first date" at the recording studio was a sign of an eventual struggle we would have as a couple with how we communicate. Though we laugh a lot now about how straightforward Judy was when expressing her romantic interest, that moment was a foreshadowing of how different our communication styles are from each other. Don't get it twisted . . . neither of us has a problem speaking our minds and cursing a bitch out if we have to, but in our relationship what we choose to communicate and when is what has caused us to lock horns.

Once Judy put her bid in to explore something beyond a professional relationship, we moved forward to the courting stage so we could get to know each other and determine whether we were a match romantically. Since we lived in different states, long distance was the only option for us to get the ball rolling. Just like other couples who are in an unfortunate situation of having miles between them, in order for us to build on our connection, the phone had to be our primary means of communication. That is, if one of us would have bothered to respond to calls and messages.

GOLDEN RULE:

"DETERMINE THE SOURCE OF THE COMMUNICATION BREAKDOWN."

Being able to express your thoughts, feelings, and needs comfortably creates feelings of closeness, mutual understanding, and trust. But there will be times when a breakdown in communication will occur. Being in a healthy, sustainable relationship doesn't mean it will be problem-free, so get that out of your head right now! Communication issues are actually pretty common even in the best of relationships. The fact that they're normal doesn't mean they don't have the potential to wreak havoc on your shit, 'cause they will. Breakdowns in communication between you and your partner can lead to more misunderstandings, arguments, and, worse, the breakup of the relationship. In order to move forward with resolving an issue, it may seem like a no-brainer, but acknowledging that there ***is*** an issue is essential. Once you and your partner are clear that something ain't right, you'll need to proceed with getting to the heart of the problem. Trust and believe the root of your communication issue will typically not be what you think it is. So you'll have to actually do a little work and delve deep into what's causing the drama. Are your communication styles polar opposites? Are there unarticulated expectations? Did one of you misunderstand something that was said? Make it a practice that both of you are clear on where the breakdown in communication is so you may work together to avoid failures in the future.

DaRealBBJudy: Let me get this out of the way. My name is Judy, and I am a phone addict. I have no problem admitting this because I know I'm not alone. Most of us live with our phones literally attached to our hip, or in my case, glued to the palm of my hand. I have a good reason for my phone addiction. I own and operate a multimillion-dollar business that continues to grow. As CEO of a small but hardworking team, there's always someone I need to text, email, FaceTime, or call about my company.

In the initial stages of my courtship with *Beaurtiful*, I relied heavily on the phone so I could get to know her more. I was based in New Orleans, and she, as the world obviously knows, is an ATL-ien. Anybody who has been in a long-distance relationship understands how vital it is for a budding couple that you talk damn near every day until you're able to be in the same place at the same time. Those daily conversations and ongoing text messages help couples bridge the gap created by distance. But what I found out was that Brat sucks at communicating by phone.

GOLDEN RULE:

"ESTABLISH BOUNDARIES."

The goal of a healthy relationship is love and mutual respect. Establishing boundaries enables each person to define what they consider to be comfortable and acceptable conduct to them. Boundaries prevent confusion, set reasonable expectations, and create an environment for a relationship to thrive because each partner is made aware of what is and isn't appropriate. Articulating your boundaries isn't easy, but trial and error is the best way to practice. Having a partner who is open and interested and cares about knowing what you think, feel, and require in the relationship is vital. If you're with someone who is dismissive of your boundaries or refuses to accept, be present, or listen as you express what's important to you, consider this a glaring red flag slapping you in the face. Another benefit of establishing firm boundaries in your relationship is that it makes each person accountable for their own feelings and actions. Boundaries are a reminder that you are not responsible for what your partner feels, the choices they make, or the things they do. Boundaries are a defined set of limits that not only teach your significant other how to treat you in the relationship but also serve as a reminder of how you must prioritize taking care of yourself.

DaRealBBJudy: When we started to get to know each other, I would send her a text to check in and ask how her day had been. Often I wouldn't get a response. Hours would go by, and I'm wondering what's going on. Brat's lapses in communication weren't just annoying, they were confusing and contradictory. I was definitely getting mixed messages. There were times when we were locked in, but then she would ghost me and I wouldn't hear from her for days at a time. I knew immediately that something wasn't right. I opted to extend her some grace because I didn't like feeling like I was intentionally being ignored.

There were also a few times during our beginning stages that *Beaurtiful* asked me to visit her in Atlanta. I would book an Airbnb and hop on a flight, and as soon as I was in the city, I'd reach out and there would be no response. Can you imagine trying to get to know someone from long distance and you make a trip to their city to see them and you get stood up? Yep. That happened.

Being a newbie to the celebrity dating game, I thought perhaps this was par for the course? Celebrity or not, I'd never experienced anything like it and had the hardest time figuring it (her) out. I noticed a pattern after a while. When she was working, we'd talk a lot. But when she got home, she wouldn't talk or respond at all to my calls or messages.

Despite her inconsistency I knew in my heart she was a nice person. I rationalized her lackluster communication to mean that she wasn't really interested in me and didn't want to tell me or didn't know how. It was clear as day that either she had something else going on or I didn't have a chance with her. So I made a decision. I wanted to get to know her, but I had to stop pursuing someone who did not want to be pursued *or* who wasn't ready to be pursued. Ultimately, I made the choice to move on and blocked her on my devices.

Though I felt rejected, I didn't walk away defeated. Besides, I'm a superoptimistic person. I wanted us to move forward, but if that was how it would be to date her, I had no other choice but to step away. I was not accustomed to having someone I'm pursuing treat my attempts to communicate with disregard. If we weren't meant to be and she wasn't the person for me, then so be it. There was no need for me to keep trying when there was no real action being taken on her part. Our energies just weren't matching. I wanted her to give back at least 70 percent of the effort that I was giving, but it wasn't happening.

GOLDEN RULE:

"TAKE PERSONAL OWNERSHIP OF YOUR ROLE IN THE PROBLEM."

Recognizing that your thoughts, words, or actions may contribute to a problem in your relationship and accepting responsibility for them is an important part of good communication. The willingness and ability to take ownership of your role in why things may have gone awry will position you and your boo to keep the issue from dragging out longer than necessary. While it's important that you both take responsibility when you mess up, you shouldn't have to do it by yourself all the time. Problems in relationships don't just appear out of nowhere. No matter how little your individual contributions may have been in a situation, you both should be capable, willing, and ready to accept responsibility when something goes wrong. When both partners are aware of how they impact the relationship, it increases the chances that whatever is going on in the relationship can be fixed pretty quickly. Another benefit of taking accountability is that it prevents negative emotions like anger and resentment from festering. A strong, long-lasting relationship needs individuals who understand the role accountability plays in the success of a partnership. Being able to be open and honest about your shortcomings demonstrates maturity, self-awareness, and a desire to relate to your loved one better.

Da Brat: I'll admit I didn't handle the beginning of our relationship well at all. What Judy didn't know at the time—and I take full responsibility for failing to communicate it to her—is that there were a few things going on. But before I delve into what was happening and why I was neglectful in responding to her texts and calls, she's totally right about one thing. I am not a fan of the phone.

What Judy didn't know was that when I put my phone down at home, I put it down and I don't look at it. There was a time when the phone had taken over my life. Every time I looked at it, there was always something or someone to respond to. My close friend Rickey Smiley, who is like a father figure to me and host of the nationally syndicated radio show *The Rickey Smiley Morning Show*, encouraged me to detach and set a boundary for myself so that I could prioritize my personal time.

I've been working in radio as a cohost of his morning show for more than eight years. Bad phone etiquette in the studio is one of his pet peeves. Whenever we are on air our phones have to be put on silent. Rickey would always talk to the team about how much phone usage was a distraction, not just while we were doing the show but during other times, too. A lot of what he has said about limiting the use of and dependence on the phone makes sense to me. So I've learned to leave my phone on silent, especially in the evenings.

It took a while for it to become second nature, but now when I get home I turn the ringer off, put the phone down on the counter, and do not look at it at all. Not answering my phone was never an issue (at least I didn't think it was) until a person came into my life who is on the phone not 24/7 but 25/8!

It was absolutely my responsibility to put my big-girl panties on and 'fess up about why I was ignoring calls and texts, but besides the phone, there was another reason. I guess I should say *reasons*. Truth be told, I was in a few romantic situations with other people. I liked Judy a lot, so I wanted to clear up my other relationships before I got seriously involved with her.

I was trying really hard to wrap up all those other situationships, but the closure wasn't happening fast enough. Plus, there were kids involved, which always makes breakups more complicated. Since I didn't say anything about what was *really* going on with me, Judy got fed up, moved on, and got a . . . boyfriend!

GOLDEN RULE:

"ACCEPT THE CONSEQUENCES."

Accepting the consequences is an important stage in the process of rebuilding a relationship, especially after a communication breakdown. Coming to grips with what has happened between you and your significant other can help you both learn to be more intentional in how you communicate. Consequences also serve as a way for you and your beloved to genuinely learn how words and actions, or the lack of both, can negatively (or positively) impact your relationship. Though repercussions should not be perceived as punishment, depending on their nature, they may feel that way. On the other hand, positive consequences can reinforce good communication habits and help strengthen your bond. It is important for the success of your relationship that consequences are dealt with in a healthy fashion. So don't pout, be angry, or argue about having to deal with them. Understanding that communication breakdowns may come with consequences, let them serve as a motivator for you and your love to work through your issues, reestablish trust if needed, and communicate better. Approaching consequences with a positive mindset can help you turn a challenge in the relationship into an opportunity to build a stronger and healthier bond.

Da Brat: What was so interesting about this situation was that I didn't tell Judy what was going on with me, and it was through social media that I found out what was going on with her and her new man! My feelings were hurt. I was like, damn, she didn't even tell me that she had given up on us. There was no "I think I'm going to move on," "it's been real," or "maybe we can link back up somewhere later in life?" Because of the way she had handled our "breakup," I proceeded with trying to reach her to find out what was going on. But I was blocked and couldn't get through to her. Had I been told she was moving on instead of finding it out on Instagram, I would have left her alone. I wouldn't have been trying to text her because I would have known she wasn't fucking with me anymore.

But I had no idea what was going on. I was blocked on the phone but not on the socials. At one point she posted a picture of herself hugged up on this dude. All you could see was the back of his head and she had her arms around him smiling and shit. I was like, okay. So she doesn't just like bitches, she likes niggas, too! How dare she go and get a boyfriend right after we had been talking? Silly me, I was busy letting people go so I could be with her. I was actively cutting motherfuckers the fuck off, and all the while she was boasting her new man on her socials? Foul on the play!

When I saw her with this dude, I was upset, disappointed, hurt, crushed, heartbroken . . . everything. But I had to deal with it. I had my own stuff that I had to take care of. I didn't like that she'd moved on, but I dealt with it and said okay, it is what it is and I'll continue on with my life. I didn't quite do that, though. I did the worst thing ever—I started stalking her Instagram.

I kept hoping this dude would not be on her page anymore and wishing they would break up. I would try not to look at her Instagram page every day. At one point I switched things up and would look maybe once a week with the hope that this dude she was with was no longer a part of her life. But there was no such luck. There would be times when she wouldn't post a picture of him and I would think they were done, but then he'd be back on the page a few days later. One time she even posted a picture of him lying in her bed! That got me heated.

I know it doesn't make much sense that I wanted her to extend me the courtesy of a heads-up when I didn't give her one, but it's how I felt (and still do). My reasons for not telling her what was going on with me had to do with my fears of losing her. If I had told her that I had some other shit going on, I just knew she would be like, *Fuck it, I'm not waiting on all that shit*. There was no guarantee that that was how she would have responded, but I wasn't willing to take the risk. It ended up happening anyway because she was posting her new man on social media, but I acknowledge that I should have spoken up.

GOLDEN RULE:

"BE HONEST ABOUT WHAT'S GOING ON."

Being honest with your significant other is definitely easier said than done, especially if it involves sharing stuff about yourself or things going on in your life that are challenging to talk about. But honesty is a big part of building and maintaining a healthy relationship, not just with someone you are involved with romantically but in all of your interpersonal relationships. Honesty sets the tone for trust and openness, which will help conflicts and misunderstandings from becoming an issue, but it also can make you feel closer to the person in your life. Embracing vulnerability and being truthful about what's going on with you is scary as fuck. But choosing to be open and giving each other permission to be seen completely, flaws and all, can help you develop a strong bond that grows into a successful relationship. It's natural to want your person to only see and know what makes you the dopest person in a room, but when you're up-front and honest, your significant other has a greater chance of understanding who you are and what you want, and, most important, it gives them the opportunity to address your needs. Honesty signals to your partner that you choose to engage with them in a manner that's transparent, trusting, and fully open in order to have a relationship built on solid ground.

Da Brat: Once Judy's relationship ended, we got back in touch with each other and after a while we made a joint decision to give our relationship another chance. I saw that as a gift. And I didn't want to screw it up. Any mistakes that I made before or dumb shit I was used to doing in relationships had to cease immediately. When you find that person and you really love them and you're not trying to let them go or mess up with them, you're going to do everything you possibly can to make sure it stays right. Being afraid to tell her the absolute truth was no longer an option. I told myself, I'm grown as hell and mature enough to be honest and up-front about everything.

What really made it possible for me to be vulnerable was Judy herself. She made me feel safe to come clean. Once I knew that she wasn't going anywhere and that I could tell her any fucking thing, I was able to share why I was distant a lot of the time.

In August 2008 I was convicted of aggravated assault and was sentenced to three years in prison. I served twenty-two months, and for the last part of my sentence I was put into a work-release program where I worked for a company that built windows. I really loved that job. And, yes, I know all about windows. During this time I fell in love with someone, but everyone doubted the relationship would work because of my celebrity and also the circumstances of how we met.

Despite the naysayers, the relationship lasted a few years after prison. We were initially friends and then moved into being a couple. I settled into this situation, and as time went on, I figured she and her kids were going to be my life, and I was okay with that until there was a major betrayal. I found out that my former partner had been sleeping with someone they had introduced me to as their friend. I also befriended this person and accepted them as part of our family. They were welcomed into our home and would come over to eat, hang out, and do all the things you do with family.

In addition to the cheating, I also found out that my former partner had other secrets and personal issues I didn't know about. I can't dive too deep into someone else's shit when this is about me and my wife, whom I love and adore, but I was really caught off guard by my former partner's betrayal and everything else I discovered about them. I couldn't believe I had no clue of what was going on, but when I think about the situation now, I was focused on getting my life back after having been in prison. Once I was in the work-release program, I was busy doing what I had to do. I went back and forth to work and performed concerts on the weekends. That was my life.

Finding out what was going on between my former partner and this "friend" turned my life upside down.

I stayed in the relationship despite the betrayal because I was concerned about her and her children. There was a lot of drama, and I didn't want to be in the relationship any longer, but I felt I had to stick around for them and their kids. So I was stuck. I couldn't abandon the people I'd grown to love even though I was betrayed in the worst way. It was a horribly complicated situation. I had met Judy and was eager to pursue things with her, but there was also this shitty situation with my ex-partner. However, being with Judy was what my heart wanted since the day we met. It just took a long time for me to figure out how to leave my previous situation.

By the time things were officially over and done with this person, Judy was with this other guy and I was stalking her Instagram hoping that relationship would end so I could have another shot with her. The only sad part is that while we're happily married now, Judy still believes that the reason why I wasn't answering my phone in the evenings was because I was with someone else, and that wasn't true. I had other situations, yes. There was also my former partner and all the issues they were dealing with. But I wasn't ignoring calls from Judy at night because I was lying up with someone else. I just don't answer my phone at night. But, more important, I was actively trying to get myself out of a complicated entanglement.

DaRealBBJudy: This is actually a point that we still talk about to this day. Brat thinks that it's because of past experiences that I feel this way, but I tell her that anybody who is dating someone and they are only available for certain hours in a day and at night they're not available, you can't help but think they've got someone else—and not that they're training themselves to stay off their phone.

Da Brat: Regardless, the bottom line for me then and now is that Judy is it for me. I'm not fucking this up. I'm doing everything right that I can because this is the person I want to be with forever. I have never felt this way and no relationship I have ever been in has been like this and I don't want to lose it.

The Takeaway

People often tell us how they really admire that we are lovers and best friends who talk to each other about everything. We have only been able to get to this place of open dialogue after stumbling our way through a few tough situations and conversations. When you're first starting out with someone or even if you've been in a relationship for a while, being vulnerable feels like a huge risk with no guarantees of a positive payoff. But keep in mind, no healthy relationship can prosper without creating an environment for openness and honesty. Here are a few more golden rules that have helped us get beyond our vulnerability fears so the lines of communication stay open, conflicts get resolved, and we both feel seen *and* heard:

1. **Check your motherfucking tone.** Undoubtedly you've heard some version of the popular expression "You catch more flies with honey than with vinegar." Another popular one is "It's not what you say, but how you say it." When it comes to effective communication with your partner, it's best to keep both of these sayings in mind because how you speak to your partner will most

certainly determine how they will respond to you. If you address someone in a tone laced with a whole lot of attitude, guess what you're sure to get in return? MORE ATTITUDE. If you've had a bad day or you're upset about something your partner has said, done, or *not* done, wait until you are able to speak to them in a nonconfrontational manner. If you're not sure what that is, think of how you would address your granny. Most of us naturally defer to a respectful tone when speaking to an elder. A patient, relaxed tone of voice with your significant other can ensure that what you have to say will actually be heard and not just responded to.

2. **Be mindful of your body language.** You can say a whole lot without verbally saying a damn thing. That's because our bodies naturally give off signals of how we feel and most times we're not even aware that we're doing it. Crossing of the arms, rolling of the eyes, turning the mouth up or other facial expressions, and tapping of the foot or fingers are a few examples of how we're communicating what we're thinking or feeling. If you're transmitting cues that you're not listening, don't care about what's being said, or think you're being attacked, your partner will pick up on it simply by how your body is responding. When communicating with your partner, make sure what's coming out of your mouth is consistent with how your body is engaging (or not) in the conversation. Make eye contact, nod to acknowledge you hear what they're saying, don't fidget or shift your weight back and forth. It may be hard to control some natural responses like yawning, especially if you're trying to hold a conversation when you're tired, but keep in mind that how you communicate with your body is just as important as what you say.

3. **Practice empathy and compassion.** If you want a relationship to go the distance, empathy and compassion must be at the heart of your day-to-day conversations and general interactions. No one wants to be involved with or married to someone who doesn't understand (or at least *try* to) when you're going through something or simply need emotional support. Knowing that you and your significant other can count on each other to listen, encourage, and be trustworthy will strengthen your connection and make communication easier and mutually beneficial.

4. **Tune in.** If you want to shut a conversation down and make someone feel unimportant, stop listening. It works every time. And, it's rude. If your partner thinks you're not listening, then you can rest assured that they're not feeling heard in the relationship. It doesn't matter if it's a conversation about the bills, the kids, or what happened at work that day. Give your partner your undivided attention. No scrolling on the phone, flipping through channels, or doing anything that takes your attention from each other. Most important, when one of you is speaking, don't interrupt or chime in with an opinion, unsolicited advice, or judgy comments. Pay attention to them as they speak and listen to hear what they are saying, not just so you can respond.

5. **Don't criticize and place blame.** No relationship can make it if you're constantly antagonizing each other with words that are critical and condemning. Instead of pointing fingers (which will automatically make them get defensive), try flipping the script and speaking to them about how their words or actions make you feel.

6. **Apologize.** If you've done or said something that was harmful, take accountability and apologize. "I'm sorry" are two simple but important words. Say them often, but also mean it. And, for goodness' sake, try not to do that shit you did over and over again.

Reflection

Da Brat

I grew up in a very loving family on the west side of Chicago. My mother and I lived with my maternal grandmother, who was saved, sanctified, and filled with the Holy Ghost. I don't remember my grandmother and grandfather ever living together, but we had a full house. My mother's sister and brother also lived with us. My grandmother ran a strict, religious household. We were in the church at least four or five days a week. It was a follow-the-straight-and-narrow-path type of home. We couldn't do shit. We would go to church and listen to church music. That's about it. I was very much an active participant in our church. I played the drums and sang in the choir. I had to wear skirts down to my ankles. I couldn't wear makeup, lipstick, heels, or toe-out shoes. I also couldn't cut my hair. All of it wasn't of God, apparently, and was too worldly. Still, I loved it.

2 Compatibility

Other than being incredibly attracted to each other, we can say without a doubt that a key ingredient in our secret sauce (and probably the reason why we have been able to build a strong-ass relationship) is that we are compatible. Basically, we are BFFs and lovers who enjoy spending time with each other, being silly, and loving on our sweet little boy, True.

That said, we don't line up on everything.

When you're starting out with someone, there's a tendency to expect that your person checks all the compatibility boxes. It's basically mandatory, otherwise what's the point, right? The good book says we should not be "unequally yoked" for a reason. It's no accident that you ask a whole bunch of questions early in a relationship in an effort to find out if you're aligned.

Do you like the same music? Do you share the same values? Do you belong to the same political party? And so on. But there's an unfortunate misconception a lot of couples believe, and that is, if your partner doesn't align with you perfectly like those couples holding up their answers on that old TV show *The Newlywed Game*, then the relationship is inevitably doomed. Please hear us and hear us clear: That's just not true.

We're not naive. We do know there are some things that are insurmountable, and trying to force a round peg into a square hole when it's clear you're not a match is akin to torture. If you're in that kind of situation, by all means, please swipe left. We've both had to do it.

GOLDEN RULE:

"DETERMINE YOUR DEAL-BREAKERS."

Deal-breakers are useful in relationships because they help shed light on underlying differences that might create problems down the road for you and your partner. In the beginning stages of a relationship, it is helpful to be aware of the things that you consider to be your deal-breakers and make sure you reveal these things to your partner. Detailing your deal-breakers can help to prevent potential conflicts or misunderstandings, but it can also help you determine whether someone is truly a match. As the slogan goes, the more you know! By identifying and communicating your deal-breakers, you can save yourself needless aggravation, heartache, or other anxiety. It is better to know up front if you are not compatible on a fundamental level than to waste time and energy in a romantic situation that's headed to splitsville. All relationships require you to put in some work, and there will be plenty of moments where you and your partner disagree, but being in a relationship with someone who is willing to compromise and come up with solutions that work for both of you is a wonderful thing. If you and your person are constantly arguing over basic values, characteristics, or behaviors, it may be a sign that the relationship is not the one, so throw up the deuces and move on. While some areas may present an opportunity for you to find the middle ground, if there are issues between you that are potentially harmful, they should be taken seriously, especially if they put your physical, mental, or emotional health at risk.

DaRealBBJudy: During one of my previous relationships, a favorite R&B singer of mine had announced concert dates in my city. I asked my partner if they would go with me. We had been a couple for quite some time. Going to a show together should not have been an issue. But they said they weren't sure if they would be able to go because they didn't have anything to wear. I didn't push the issue. I opted not to go. I should have gone to the concert anyway, but I really wanted to go with the one I loved. Silly me.

I ended up with egg on my face because I found out later that my partner did go to the concert but with someone else! When I asked them about going to the show without me, they came up with some excuse about their friend having an extra ticket so they took them up on their offer. I know it was all bullshit even if the friend was platonic. Still, it was inconsiderate shit like that time and again in this former relationship and others that helped me determine that being inconsiderate is a deal-breaker for me.

Despite realizing that my former partner and I were incompatible, I tried to stick it out with them as long as possible even though I was truly miserable. I couldn't even be around my children because I was so unhappy. I would close the door to my room and avoid them. It wasn't that I didn't love them. I just didn't want to expose them to the gloomy energy that being in that relationship had me feeling. I love my kids more than anything, but while in that relationship I often would choose to not interact with them because I was miserable.

Misery for a normally optimistic person is like being killed slowly. There was only so much my happy-go-lucky, Positive Patty self could deal with. When things failed to get better, I did the unthinkable. Yes, I cheated. I am ashamed. Well, not really. Okay, maybe a little bit.

My partner found out about it while we were on a family vacation in the most unoriginal way possible: My phone was unlocked, and they went through it. Let me tell you this—there is nothing like having a major relationship crisis while you're on a vacation far from home and you can't escape your partner!

I know I should not have cheated, but I wasn't strong enough to walk away. I was looking for love outside of the relationship since I wasn't getting any love in it. My former partner and I eventually broke up. What I can say is that our breakup wasn't because I didn't think they loved me. I wholeheartedly believe they did. We just weren't right for each other. So again, if that's you and you're in a horrible-ass relationship, don't just casually walk to the door. . . . Sprint and get out!

GOLDEN RULE:

"SEEK AREAS OF COMMON GROUND."

Because it provides a foundation for communication and other key aspects of a romantic relationship, discovering common ground is an important component of compatibility. Since no two people are alike, it's wise to have reasonable expectations; yet, discovering shared interests can definitely enrich your connection. Additionally, common ground leads to a great deal of intimacy and closeness because it confirms that you and your partner are on the same page, making it easier to understand each other. This shared understanding can help you navigate challenges better because it creates a sense of unity and teamwork within the relationship. Overall, having things you and your significant other enjoy and value together can bring joy and fulfillment to your relationship, deepen your bond, and help you create lasting memories. While opposing viewpoints and hobbies definitely add some spice to a relationship, they also increase the likelihood of conflict. When two people have similar interests, beliefs, and aspirations, they are more likely to be able to weather storms together, which builds the foundation for a long-term partnership. You don't have to have a laundry list of things, but even a few areas of common ground can make a big difference in your relationship.

DaRealBBJudy: But back to my *Beaurtiful*. . . . I remember at one point early on in our relationship I asked what her five-year goals were. I wanted to know what she was thinking, what she wanted to do, and where she wanted to end up. In addition to being optimistic, I am totally goal-oriented. I was eager to see if *Beaurtiful* and I were like-minded in that way. But she didn't have an answer for me.

I'll never forget when we were on a plane and I asked her that same question again. The second time around, she snapped back, "Maybe I'm not the right person for you because you keep asking me this and I don't have an answer." I didn't understand why she didn't know. All my life that's what I have known. It's what I do—set goals. So I didn't understand why she didn't.

GOLDEN RULE:

"BE FLEXIBLE."

A certain degree of adaptability is necessary for the success of a relationship. In order for your bond to continue to develop and flourish, it is essential that you and your partner are able to adapt to changes and explore your differences without all hell breaking loose. Practicing flexibility in a relationship does not mean sacrificing your own personal ideals. It does, however, require compromise and a willingness to accept that it's okay for your partner to have a different perspective than yours. Your relationship stands a better chance of blossoming healthily when there's an atmosphere where both of you can be who you are, be seen and heard, and feel valued despite your different choices, viewpoints, or actions.

DaRealBBJudy: As I got to learn more about *Beaurtiful*, I realized that she's experienced so much life, so early and so fast. I discovered the reason she doesn't have the same desire to map out goals is because she's already done a lot of things that I'm busy planning to do (at some point). For a person like me who is all about meeting business goals, *Beaurtiful*'s reaction to my question forced me to look at things from her perspective instead of mine. Because she sees that my tendency is to plan so much that I can miss out on the present moment, she pushes me to take a break and prioritize spending time with my family. She encourages me to sit down, slow down, and just be.

Another way our differences play out is if something happens or someone upsets *Beaurtiful*, she'll harp on it and try to figure out every aspect of why this was said or that was done. Because she's preoccupied and frustrated, something else will inevitably happen, like the milk for our son gets spilled. Then another thing happens to pile on top of the other things. Suddenly, instead of having a bad moment, it turns into *Beaurtiful* having a bad day.

I believe couples pick up traits from their significant others. That is certainly true for us. Unfortunately there are times when I pick up on her pessimism. In order for me to thrive and to live, I have to think the best no matter how the situation looks. While we absolutely draw out the best in each other, a lesson that has taken root in us about compatibility is that for her to be comfortable in her space, she cannot take part in the practices that I do. And in order for me to be comfortable in my space, I cannot take part in the practices that she does. Basically, constant optimism is not something that she is comfortable with and negative thinking is not something that works for me.

Da Brat: I wouldn't say that I'm a negative person, but I'm very quick to take something the wrong way. I'm naturally defensive about everything. I always have a guard up. Anytime anyone says something to me, I will look at them sideways to see if they are being smart or have an ulterior motive. When you've been in the recording industry for as long as I have, you grow a tough outer shell because the industry is notorious for chewing folks up and spitting them out. Remember A Tribe Called Quest's Rule 4080? Well, it's true. Record company people **are** shady. All those years of being around people who lied, mistreated me, and misused me had a huge impact on my outlook on things and also my moods.

DaRealBBJudy: One of my favorite sayings is "All will be well," especially if you believe it. Everything will work out for the greater good. I'm not a Pollyanna all the time, but I do believe when you aren't positive you get exactly what you think. I will always lean toward a positive outlook, but that's where Brat and I are completely different.

GOLDEN RULE:

"FIND AN APPRECIATION FOR YOUR DIFFERENCES."

Recognizing and, more important, embracing your differences will help you develop a long-lasting relationship. Learning to see your contrasting viewpoints as something valuable in your lives rather than a source of contention can significantly improve the capacity for you and your partner to get along with, love, and support each other. Your opposing perspectives can serve as motivation for you both to strive harder to understand each other. Being difficult or unwilling to embrace differences can lead to missing out on learning something new or considering an alternative viewpoint that could actually impact your life in a positive way. There will certainly be times when you and your partner will disagree and struggle to understand each other, but a partnership built on respect, honesty, and empathy will be better suited to handle these obstacles. Recognizing and accepting that you don't see things the same way all the time can actually be a superpower in your relationship and help to strengthen your connection. Allowing space for your differences to exist without them causing strife will make the relationship more interesting and most definitely rewarding. Remember that the goal is not to avoid arguments. It's okay to disagree, but when you do, treat each other's perspectives with respect and understanding.

Da Brat: What I love about my wife is how different we are in the way we deal with things. While our approaches are often contrasting, I am willing to watch, listen, and learn. Sometimes I don't want to, but she's supersmart and makes a lot of sense about so many things. Having her in my life as my wife and partner definitely makes me a better person. No one else in the world has been able to get me to admit that. That's because she's magic.

Being in love with someone I don't always agree with has allowed me to put my guard down and be vulnerable and learn new things. It's enabled me to truly let Judy into my heart and even accept criticism from her because I know she genuinely loves me. There's a whole bunch of people who will tell you that I am a changed woman thanks to her. I was the type of person where you couldn't tell me shit before. I didn't trust anybody. But I trust my wife.

• • •

While the degree to which you and your partner are compatible will play a significant role in whether you are able to build a lasting, fulfilling relationship together, the willingness to experience new things or consider different perspectives will help to keep the relationship fresh. It also adds something else to the list of things that you and your partner can explore together.

DaRealBBJudy: In the beginning, *Beaurtiful* didn't just hate the phone and texting, she hated taking photos and recording videos. Anything that had to do with the phone she disliked. Plus, she was still in the closet. I'm pretty sure she was wondering why I was always videoing and taking photos. It certainly wasn't to expose her or the relationship. I just understand how beneficial phone devices and apps can be.

For me, one of the biggest advantages of having a smartphone is being able to take photos and videos of memorable moments. I was in New Orleans when Hurricane Katrina happened. Like many people, I lost a lot of keepsakes because the hurricane wiped everything out. I am more conscious about documenting everything now because of this. Also, we are in the content era. I want to make sure that I capture as many memories as I can via social media. Instagram, TikTok, Snap, and sites like them are not without issues, but I can positively say that social media has had a huge impact on my life and the growth of my company.

Being in a relationship with someone who has some disdain for something you do or like can potentially cause friction, but I knew I could get *Beaurtiful* to come around and see the value in the things I enjoy that she had come to dislike.

Da Brat: They say when you become a celebrity you'll never ever be left alone because the minute you are recognized, everyone will ask for photos and autographs and shit. And it's true. Throughout my career I would get bombarded with people wanting to take pictures of me everywhere I went. If it wasn't a fan, it was paparazzi. It got to the point that I didn't want to take any more pictures because it got on my damn nerves. On top of that, when Judy and I became a thing, I wasn't out of the closet so I just wanted to chill with her and not worry about capturing anything or being seen by anyone.

DaRealBBJudy: I knew my constant picture and video taking frustrated her, so there were times when I wouldn't bother to record or snap photos. Of course, those were always the times when something memorable would happen. To this day I regret that I have nothing to look back on from the time *Beaurtiful* planned and cooked her first romantic meal for me. She shopped for all the ingredients, spent all this time cooking, but I never got to taste a bite of the food.

Da Brat: What had happened was . . . I wanted to make an impression and cook for Judy. I had purchased these two amazing steaks. They were so big and juicy. I can't even remember what type of cut they were. All I know is that the steaks were good grades of meat and expensive. I went to Whole Foods to get some good cooking wine to use with the steaks. I had everything I needed for my side, which was my special cauliflower dish that everyone loves.

I seasoned the steaks and put them in the refrigerator to marinate in the cooking wine that Whole Foods employees recommended. After a while I put the steaks in the oven to cook. When I did a taste test of the meat, it was bitter and disgusting! It was truly the nastiest shit I had ever tasted. Those fuckers at Whole Foods recommended the wrong wine! I was so upset. I threw those expensive cuts of meat in the trash. There was no way I was going to let Judy's first impression of me cooking for her be that I made some nasty-tasting food. Nope.

DaRealBBJudy: *Beaurtiful* was so angry that she wouldn't even let me take a bite. She immediately put the steaks in a trash bag and ran out and threw the food down the trash chute. It was a hilarious moment and one of those instances that you just wish you had a photo or a video of to keep as a memory. But it was so early on in our relationship, and she was not comfortable with me documenting everything.

It took *Beaurtiful* about a year to get accustomed to me being preoccupied with capturing our special moments and creating content for my company. I made the most headway when

I showed her the real-time financial impact of a Kaleidoscope post to help push sales of my products.

One day she was frustrated and felt that I was on my phone for too long and not paying her any attention. I told her that I was about to announce a sale in my online store. When I pushed the post live, I wanted her to see the effect of the post. I sat next to her and we watched the numbers increase by the thousands within minutes. I remember saying to her, "This is how these things connect."

Da Brat: Because we weren't initially compatible in this area, it was a process for me to get used to the role the phone and social media play in Judy's personal life and business. Eventually I started posting more myself. I'm in no way addicted to it as she is, but I have been posting and picking up my phone more. The majority of the time, my phone still stays on silent, unless I'm away from her.

The Takeaway

Our goal as a couple has been to cultivate a loving relationship that lasts. We are aligned on some things, but in the areas where we aren't, we forge ahead by leaning into love and respect and trying our best to see things from the other person's perspective. As we grow together one of our biggest discoveries has been that what makes people compatible isn't only the things that you have in common. What we've learned is that compatibility often comes in the form of how you meet each other's needs in order to stay emotionally and romantically aligned. Whether it's anticipating what would make your partner feel loved and supported or simply making an effort to understand a different perspective than your own, to be truly compatible is to be open to strengthening your bond in a variety of ways. Here are a few more golden rules to keep in mind about compatibility:

1. **It's okay to split if you just don't fit.** They say everything ain't for everybody. The same holds true for people. Do yourself a favor and don't prolong your stay in a relationship if you don't see eye to eye about the things that are most important to you. If you're having trouble relating to each other on critical issues, swipe left and keep it pushing. You'll be saving yourself from future frustration and heartbreak if you rip the Band-Aid off quickly and nip things in the bud before getting *too* involved.

2. **Chemistry does not mean compatibility.** Physical attraction is an important factor in a relationship, but it can't be the only thing you have. The sexual energy you feel with someone is needed to set things off, but compatibility is what the relationship will be built on. Do you have common values, interests, and goals? If a lasting relationship is what you desire, chemistry will only take you so far. Besides, looks and sexual desire can fade. But sharing common ground on the things that are important in your life will make spending time together in and out of the sack much more enjoyable.

3. **Your authentic self is enough.** You shouldn't have to fake the funk to keep someone interested, so don't go changing to try and please them. Be honest about who you are, your beliefs, and your desires. Show up as yourself at all times so you can build a relationship on truth and acceptance.

3 Fight Fair

Question: What do you get when two dynamic, passionate, opinionated, take-no-shit types of women become a couple?

Answer: Some really spicy arguments!

And we have had a few. Thankfully, there haven't been that many. It's because we are honestly committed to making our relationship work. No relationship is without disagreements, but we really don't like to fight. We're so much better at loving each other. Seriously. Also, the idea of a simple disagreement becoming a knockdown, drag-out verbal fisticuffs where we're each trying to one-up the other over some bullshit really doesn't appeal to us. Words hurt just as much as punches do. So we aim to keep cool heads the majority of the time.

As we shared in the compatibility chapter, our approaches to some things definitely differ, but when it comes to fighting, we practice as best as we can to communicate civilly. When or if things get heated, we avoid going for each other's jugular. Nothing good can *ever* come from that. So our motto is to fight fair. We succeed most of the time, but there was a situation where things got slightly out of hand (and thrown across the room).

GOLDEN RULE:

"PINPOINT WHY YOU'RE MAD."

When you are angry, it can be difficult to think clearly and rationally. You may lash out at your partner or say a whole bunch of stuff you don't mean or really shouldn't even say in the first place. Taking the time to identify the root of your anger can help you calm down and approach the situation in a more constructive and productive way. By pinpointing the specific reasons for what has gotten you hot under the collar, you can also prevent misunderstandings and miscommunications from escalating into a bigger problem. Being clear about the source of your frustration allows you to express your feelings in a more organized and coherent manner, which can lead to a more meaningful exchange. It's totally normal to get in your feelings about something your honey did/didn't do or say. The important thing is to understand what's fueling the emotion so you can articulate what's bothering you more effectively and resolve the conflict quickly so that it doesn't damage your relationship.

DaRealBBJudy: Welp. *Beaurtiful* got her phone broken. And no, it wasn't because of cheating. We have never had anything like that.

Let me go all the way back to the beginning. I was in a relationship with someone previously, and this person stayed in contact with all of their exes. They thought it was cool for them to be friends with people they used to be intimate with, but I didn't. When *Beaurtiful* and I got together, we had a conversation about what would and would not be acceptable in the relationship. Because I didn't like how it made me feel when a former partner would communicate with their exes, I told *Beaurtiful* that that was definitely a no-no. To me, once you've broken up and moved on with someone else, there's no need for any communication with a former partner. There should be no "I love yous," "I miss yous," or even "How was your day?" Communicating with someone you've been intimate with in the past should be off-limits so neither person will be enticed to take a stroll down the horizontal memory lane.

GOLDEN RULE:

"SET THE RULES OF THE RELATIONSHIP."

When it comes to disagreements, having ground rules can help prevent arguments from escalating and becoming destructive. You may have a tendency to want to knock all your shit over when you are in a fight, but for the sake of your relationship, it's better that you don't. Making sure there are rules for your disagreements, as well as in the relationship in general, can help you clarify expectations, prevent misunderstandings, and de-escalate conflict by giving both of you a sense of control. Deciding that you will use respectful language in the argument and not call each other out of your names (so no *bitch ass, motherfucka,* and *triflin' ass ho* would be allowed) or going to separate rooms when things get truly heated are types of rules you may choose to implement. Setting rules can also make sure you and your partner work to repair the relationship in a healthy manner once things have calmed down. Keep in mind that your rules should not be too rigid or inflexible but tailored to the relationship and how you interact with each other. Also, it's important for you both to understand that as the relationship grows and evolves, so should your rules. By establishing clear and workable guidelines for disagreements, you and your partner can create a more positive and productive way of handling your conflicts.

DaRealBBJudy: Since we openly communicate about everything, *Beaurtiful* now (as opposed to when we first started) has no problem telling me things. She'll say "so and so" texted or called me today. There was one time when she told me she had heard from someone that I knew was an ex. I didn't like that she was texting with them, but I opted to sit back and see how far their chatting was gonna go. To her credit, I did appreciate that she shared that she was in communication with them, but from my standpoint it was still a violation of our rules because I talked about this being one of the things I felt was unacceptable.

Their texting continued until one day while looking at her phone (yes, we have access to each other's devices) I saw that she had texted this person that they had "pretty feet." I immediately went to *Beaurtiful* and said, "You told somebody you used to sleep with that they have pretty feet?" Our disagreement started right after that.

Often when we are in a fight, and it doesn't matter what the issue is, *Beaurtiful* will want to make her points and defend herself. When I feel she is talking but not listening or understanding what I'm saying, my approach is to turn the situation around to get her to see the situation from my point of view. But I lost my cool, and I hurled her phone across the room first.

Not my best moment, I know, but I really had her attention after she saw her phone get tossed. I then asked her how she would feel if I told someone I had been intimate with that one of their body parts was cute?

GOLDEN RULE:

"TRY TO UNDERSTAND EACH OTHER'S PERSPECTIVE."

Creating a healthy environment for your relationship to succeed requires that you and your partner try to understand each other, especially during disagreements. Striving to see each other's perspective can help you become more empathetic and compassionate toward each other, leading to clearer and more efficient communication. The goal isn't to determine who is right but to minimize the conflict by giving each other space to express yourselves, listening to what each other has to say, and then finding common ground. Understanding why your partner feels the way they do can help you react less defensively and proactively work toward a compromise or, even better, a resolution.

Da Brat: My answer was that I probably wouldn't appreciate it and would wonder why she was telling them something like that. But let's backtrack. Though Judy says we talked about it, I don't think we did because I didn't know it wasn't okay. Also, I see this issue differently. I feel as long as there ain't nothing going on and you're not sexually involved or anything like that, you should be able to communicate by text or even talk with an ex. Regardless, I did understand where she was coming from and how it made her feel.

At the same time, I felt that if it was her talking to an ex and innocent banter was how they communicated with each other, I wouldn't think anything of it. I would trust that nothing is going on. More important, I would trust her. I really don't think exes talking to each other is an issue, but my baby did so I nipped that communication in the bud immediately.

It's been a few years since we had this fight, and this is still a topic that we don't fully agree about. I completely understand and respect her feelings, but I really don't think she should have thrown my phone. I know she was upset when she did it, but my perspective on the text hasn't changed. It was harmless. It wasn't like I was saying to them, *I want to have sex with you.* I made an innocent comment about their feet, and I don't think my phone deserved to be broken because of it.

When you are in a disagreement with the one you love, you have to be willing to compromise. If it's not cool with my wife, then I have to agree: It's not cool. My text about my ex's feet made my baby feel a certain way. She made that loud and clear and definitely got my attention when she threw the phone. I knew I had to take appropriate action and stop communicating with my ex because the one thing that was going through my head after the phone went flying across the room was *This bitch is crazy*, and I better go block this ex for the rest of my life!

GOLDEN RULE:

"TAKE A TIME-OUT IF NECESSARY."

During a disagreement, prioritize taking a break to prevent things from escalating. Breaks will give you and your partner time to breathe, remember why you love each other, and get your head right. It's difficult to calm yourself down when you're caught in a heated back-and-forth. Taking some space allows you to collect your thoughts and return to the conversation with a fresh (and calmer) perspective. Stepping away from a conflict temporarily will help you protect the bond you share with your partner. It also reduces the likelihood of either one of you saying or doing something hurtful, as upset people are more likely to say things they don't mean and regret later. Disagreements are normal parts of any relationship, but taking a break during an extremely heated situation will enable you both to come back to the drawing board (hopefully) less stressed and willing to communicate with each other clearly in order to preserve and strengthen the relationship rather than tearing it down.

DaRealBBJudy: I probably shouldn't have let my emotions get the best of me, but seeing that "pretty toes" text made me think *Beaurtiful* was still cleaning up her other situations, and she was supposed to have been way past that since our relationship had progressed significantly. We weren't just talking to each other on the phone anymore. We went from me traveling back and forth to see her, to me moving to Atlanta, to us looking at houses, to buying a house and then moving in together. *Beaurtiful* said all of her prior situations had been cleared up, but that text gave me vibes that things with this former lover weren't resolved although she said they were.

Reacting in anger definitely wasn't cool, but one thing I truly admire about how *Beaurtiful* handles disagreements is (1) she is 1,000 percent more mature than me. I have no problem admitting that. (2) No matter how angry or upset we both are, she is always the first one to communicate, apologize, and want to talk things through. I'm the complete opposite.

When I'm superangry to the point where I look like the angry emoji with steam coming out of my face, I don't like to talk because I can turn into someone who's not a true representation of who I am. Many people say and do hurtful things when they are mad. I am not normally one of those people, but I can become one quickly.

It doesn't matter who I'm fighting with; if things have gotten really heated and I want to get a lick in, believe me when I say that I know exactly how to bring a person to their knees. But because my relationship with *Beaurtiful* is sacred, I always want to fight fair. Instead of allowing myself a moment to get revenge or say something in anger that I won't be able to take back, I'd rather walk away, take some time, and then talk about it with her later after I've calmed down. *Beaurtiful* thinks it's selfish to not talk when an olive branch has been extended. I don't agree. I believe you resolve things better when cool heads prevail. With the exception of the phone-throwing incident, our disagreements don't get very intense, and I'm really grateful for that.

GOLDEN RULE:

"DON'T TAKE YOUR FRUSTRATION OUT ON EACH OTHER."

It is completely unacceptable to take your frustrations out on your significant other. Whether you're in the middle of an argument or not, this type of behavior is abusive and a surefire way to ruin your relationship. In the heat of the moment, animosity and resentment may build, but your partner should never be on the receiving end of any hostility you feel. Taking your anger out on each other creates a toxic environment that is devoid of communication, respect, and trust. It also increases the risk of physical violence, stress, or depression, because no one wants to be the dumping ground for someone else's frustration. Instead, it's essential to find more constructive ways to manage your frustration before things escalate. If treating your partner respectfully is no longer possible, dissolving the relationship is always the most mature and responsible choice.

Da Brat: Just like any other couple, the topics of our disagreements depend on the situation. Most of our fights are because of something to do with our reality show. But normally if we're not vibing with each other, it is because one of us is in a funky mood. I could be annoyed about something that happened or irritable from work, and Judy will say, "Why are you talking to me like that? What's wrong with you?"

That's usually my cue to check myself and fix my attitude. When she's angry or frustrated, I do the same. I remind her not to speak to me in a crazy tone. If we're both in a mood, we'll opt to take space from each other and go to separate corners of the house. After we both have had a mood adjustment, we'll come back together.

DaRealBBJudy: There was one time in our relationship I was so angry that I got in my car and just left. I don't remember where I told *Beaurtiful* I was going, but I drove to New Orleans from Atlanta. I just had to get away because once again we were in a situation where I felt there were signs that her prior situations were not totally resolved, and I was pissed. What set me off was *Beaurtiful* told me she was shutting that other relationship down, but she gave that woman a car! That didn't seem right to me. If you're in a relationship with someone, things are supposed to be ending, and you're splitting your possessions, then ain't no way in the world are you gonna give that person a car. There were a lot of different things with that relationship that made me feel like something wasn't right. *Beaurtiful* and I had bought our house and all of her things were physically there, but it didn't feel like she was clear about her future with me. I didn't like feeling like I forced her to do all these things with me if she wasn't completely done with her other situation. I decided I'd rather be elsewhere as she figured it out. So I left.

Da Brat: I hadn't heard from Judy in days. I was in this big-ass house all by myself. I was calling my friends in tears. My friends were considering doing a wellness check on me because I was losing it. My baby was gone. I didn't know where she was, and she wasn't trying to speak to me! I thought I was dying. I finally got a text from Judy, and she said she was in New Orleans. I couldn't believe she just up and drove all the way to New Orleans. I thought she was fucking going to get some fresh air and to just get out the house. But she drove her ass to another city! I was sick about it. I was throwing up. Judy leaving had really fucked me up. When I'd ask when she was coming back, she wouldn't give me an answer. So I got me a flight and hotel room and headed down there to look for her.

Now, I'm a celebrity. I never do any shit like that by myself. I always roll with someone because people will fuck with you when they see that you're alone. But I big-girled it and got on a fucking plane to go get my baby back. I stayed at the Roosevelt hotel. I thought it was a sweet gesture because that's where we ended up meeting up when I was in New Orleans for the 2019 Essence Festival. I had it all worked out. I texted Judy and told her where I was and that I had the same room from the last time I stayed there. But she didn't respond. I woke up the next morning and found out that she was back in Atlanta! She drove her ass back home while I was sitting in this hotel room in New Orleans. That entire situation was the worst for me. I felt like my heart was breaking. I could barely breathe. The mere thought that things had gotten to that point was unbearable to me.

DaRealBBJudy: When we had our discussion about all that she had going on, I asked *Beaurtiful* to get it cleared up. I gave her the freedom, space, and time to take care of what she needed. She had months. I didn't hound her about it. But we were in a fucking house together by that point and from my perspective there shouldn't have been much more left for her to resolve. It was clear to me that if she was going to be "cleaning up" things from her prior relationship for several damn years, then she and I had a major problem in our relationship because that wasn't part of the plan. Once I learned she had given her ex a car, that was it for me.

Da Brat: I let my former partner have the car because they had a kid and the kid was in school. They needed to be able to drive them around.

GOLDEN RULE:

"DON'T GO TO BED ANGRY."

Going to bed angry is never a good idea. Not only can it lead to resentment and bitterness, but it also clearly signals a breakdown in communication. Taking your anger to bed is like putting a wall up between you and your partner, making it even harder to hash things out if you're both still seething about an issue that happened the day before. To foster a healthier environment, aim to settle a conflict before retiring for the night. If you are too tired to talk, make sure you both agree on a specific time to revisit the issue. Whether the conversation happens later that night or first thing in the morning, you and your partner must be willing to listen to each other's perspective. Once you both have had the opportunity to express your feelings, work toward a resolution with compromise being your objective. In many cases, one or both of you may have to let something go in order to prioritize the relationship and the argument can come to an end.

Da Brat: A rule I am adamant that we never break is going to bed angry at each other. Some people lay their head down at night and never wake up again, so I don't like for us to go to bed without resolving any issues between us. I also don't like holding grudges. Judy is very good at not speaking when she's mad. She could not talk to me all damn day and be fine. I don't like it, but I understand she needs to take the time to cool off. As someone who was known as a hothead and even went to prison for it, I have to respect when my wife needs space.

I've never in my life put up with shit from anyone, but love really does change you. Judy is the only one who can talk to me in any kind of way (or not talk to me when she's mad). I often have to laugh. If it were anyone else in the world saying something to me that I don't like, I would have punched them in the throat in no time. But I'm not that way with my baby. I listen to what she has to say. If I've done something to upset her, I make sure I apologize and do my best to clear the air between us quickly. And, if I don't want any problems or phones thrown across the room, I make sure I don't text any exes.

The Takeaway

If you're heading into a relationship expecting that everything will be roses and sunshine every day, get ready for your much-needed reality check: You and your partner are gonna fight. Deal with it. Not every fight is an indication that a relationship is inherently doomed. The intensity and frequency of arguments may be a predictor that it's in your best interest to go your separate ways, but a disagreement here and there does not mean the end is near. However, fighting fair is a foolproof way to make sure your relationship doesn't drift into the toxic zone. Here are a few more helpful golden rules to keep your disagreements with your significant other focused, civil, and productive:

1. **Stick to the issue.** Emotions can get heightened during a fight, but don't lose sight of what you're actually in disagreement about. Bringing other topics into the fray will add to both of your frustrations because you won't be able to get anywhere. The fight just becomes a variety of grievances, which makes it difficult to get to a resolution or compromise. Stay focused on the topic.

2. **Pay attention to your own tendencies.** If you make a habit of using arguments to control your partner—such as raising your voice in an intimidating way or using swear words during

the argument—you likely turn disagreements into fights. A disagreement is when two people see things differently. A fight is when one person attacks another or both attack each other. If you shut down during arguments by refusing to communicate or walking out of the room, it can rile up your partner—who now likely feels disrespected—and put resolution at a further distance. Incoming truth bomb . . . it's time to grow up! Learn to come to a disagreement with love, respect, and honesty. But first, identify your triggers, then ask yourself if they help during an argument. Finally, shed the tendencies that don't serve you, your partner, or the relationship.

3. **Revisit the rules.** You and your partner should have relationship ground rules. The rules are meant to keep you both accountable and establish boundaries. When you're in a fight, an important step you should not overlook is the ground-rule check-in. Were rules broken or boundaries crossed? If the answer is yes, remind your partner that they agreed to the rules. Then ask if they still believe in them. If their answer is yes, then an apology is in order. But it shouldn't stop there. Apologies are words, but to preserve or grow trust, actions need to back those words up.

   Side note: If your partner no longer agrees to previously set boundaries, the best possible scenario is that they'll come clean and tell you so. It takes a lot of maturity to say, "I know I told you that I agree we should xyz, but I no longer want to be held to that." It takes even more maturity to hear those words and understand that the rules have now changed. What to do next is up to you. If your goal is building a relationship that lasts, you'll need to decide if you want to be with someone who doesn't want to abide by the rules you set for your partnership.

4. **Take off your armor.** Armor is for battle, and a disagreement with the one you love doesn't have to be a war. If you're engaging in an argument beneath layers of protection, you're not only making yourself unreachable, you're not reaching out. You're guaranteeing that neither a resolution nor a compromise will be reached. There are a couple of reasons you might put up barriers of defense when you disagree. One could be that you're intimidated by your partner. Another could be that you're replaying the way conflict happened in your home when you were a kid. Or, it could be both. Whatever it is, that armor is robbing you of your freedom of expression and your ability to connect.

5. **Stay away from the insults.** You undoubtedly have a few zingers in your back pocket that you're prepared to unleash on your partner if they say something you don't like. If you take no other advice we offer, do take this one: DON'T DO IT. Once those insults come out of your mouth, there ain't no turning back. You and your partner are going to fight—but remember to fight about an issue and not each other.

6. **Don't be passive-aggressive.** If your partner has done or said something that has angered or frustrated you, own your feelings. Say what's bothering you. Don't resort to passive-aggressive behaviors like sulking, slamming doors and cabinets, giving the silent treatment, or lacing your conversations with venom. Use.

Your. Words. If you're gonna fight or disagree, at least make sure your significant other must reckon with the actual problem. Don't put them in the position of having to read your mind. Talk yo shit!

7. **Don't yell and talk over each other.** Nobody likes to be yelled at. Yes, you're angry, but the minute you start yelling, your partner is sure to respond in kind. The easiest way to get your point across and to make sure you are heard is to keep your voice at a respectful tone. Yelling and screaming at each other doesn't solve anything. It just makes the neighbors want to call the cops on y'all.

8. **Keep your hands to yourself.** That is it. That is all.

Reflection

DaRealBBJudy

Someone once told me that a child will either reject or move away from what they experienced during their upbringing or mimic it. My parents raised my siblings and me in a loving home in New Orleans, Louisiana. We didn't have a lot, but we weren't poor. We were definitely rich with love because my parents told us they loved us every day. Since my dad was big on family events, every Sunday he made sure that we went on a family outing. We would go to the park, go eat beignets, or ride our bikes.

Among the many memories we made as a family, what I remember the most is how my mom and dad used to love each other. My dad was the breadwinner in our family, and because my parents were old-school, my mom did all the housework. She would make every meal, fix my dad a plate, bring his plate to him, take the plate from him when he was finished, then wash all the dishes.

4 Trust

When it became clear to us that this love thing had bitten us both something hard, we'd often forget to hide it. In public, we'd instinctively reach for each other's hands, totally forgetting that Brat had not made a formal "announcement" to tell the world (as if it's any of their business) that she likes women. The idea that a press conference or some shit like that would need to happen before we could engage in something so wonderful and natural like public displays of affection was ridiculous.

But the rumor mill was buzzing about us. We didn't have an Olivia Pope–type fixer to help us navigate the paparazzi waiting in the wings to capture a "gotcha" moment to confirm the suspected. We just focused on loving each other and building our trust bond until Brat was able and willing to own her truth in front of the world.

GOLDEN RULE:

"THERE IS NO VULNERABILITY WITHOUT TRUST."

Superstar author Brené Brown said it best: "There is no vulnerability without trust." In other words, you can't (or won't) be open and honest with your partner if you don't trust them. Not only do trust and vulnerability go hand in hand, but they are also the building blocks for intimacy and connection in a relationship. To be vulnerable, both you and your partner must commit to creating a safe space where you're both able to be yourselves and express your most intimate feelings without fear of judgment or rejection. Because trust builds over time, if you're in a new relationship, being honest, reliable, respectful, and empathetic are simple ways to show that you are trustworthy. So be intentional about your actions. Once trust is established, you and your love can continue to draw closer in an environment where you both feel loved, supported, respected, and valued for who you are and what you bring to the relationship.

Da Brat: The scrutiny and invasion of privacy that came with my rap career was intense. I have been a tomboy my entire life, and people speculated that I was gay, but I always had boyfriends. I got involved in my first same-sex relationship at the start of my career in the early to mid-1990s. My album *Funkdafied* had been released, and I was just coming into my fame and sexuality.

There was something so amazing about being in my first relationship with a woman. But whenever someone asked who my girlfriend was, I would automatically say she was my "best friend." Of course, back then I couldn't say who she really was. At that time, same-sex relationships were taboo in both the hip-hop and the Black communities. There was no way I could live as an "out Black artist" despite the fact that there were rumors that I was gay. I knew better than to say anything that would confirm the gossipers. Coming out would have been career suicide.

If a white woman like Ellen DeGeneres could have her career snatched away because she came out of the closet, I could only imagine what would happen to me. I was nowhere near as big of a celebrity as Ellen, but watching the fallout she faced when she simply wanted to be herself made me more determined to stay my ass in the closet and in my bubble of privacy in order to protect myself, my private life, and the career I was working so hard to build.

I was with my first girlfriend for about two years. The threat of potential consequences for coming out (or worse, being outed) pushed me further into the closet. I never spoke about my private life to anyone, not even with members of my family—especially my churchgoing maternal grandmother. I couldn't tell my family that the woman who was with me all the time whom I called my "best friend" was actually my girlfriend.

I believe my father's side of the family knew I was in this relationship, but no one said anything. They just loved and supported me. I dared not bring my girlfriend around my superreligious grandmother. It didn't matter if I called her my best friend or not.

She wouldn't have approved. I was heartbroken that I could not be up-front and honest with her and other loved ones about my sexuality, but the consequences of coming out felt like too much of a risk to take.

Any person in a public-facing field like the entertainment industry opens themselves up to being scrutinized by strangers who feel they have the right to judge and say whatever they want about you. I knew that if I kept things private, those comments, opinions, and anything else people had to say would only be based on speculation. Also, as a woman in the music industry, for my star to keep rising and to grow my fan base, I had to appear "fuckable." I couldn't come out and say I had a boyfriend, much less a girlfriend. The objective for so many female artists (and it's still that way) is to make the public want to know more about you and feel like they have a chance to be you or be *with* you. Keeping the media and my fans curious helped to drive album sales and sold tickets to shows.

Shielding my sexuality from the public while trying to find love and maintaining relationships as the media wanted to know every detail about me was incredibly stressful. I know I wasn't the only Black lesbian celebrity back then, but it sure felt like it. In spite of the challenge to safeguard my privacy, I am fortunate to have been able to accomplish a lot of things that I am truly proud of—movie roles, sold-out tours around the world, red-carpet appearances—but I did all those things while hiding the most authentic part of myself: the way I love. That is, until Judy. Not only did I find love, but in her I found someone I could trust implicitly who encouraged me to step out of the closet.

GOLDEN RULE:

"TAKE A RISK TOGETHER."

An intimate relationship rooted in trust, open dialogue, and mutual support can thrive when you and your partner opt to step outside of your respective comfort zones to take a bold step together or explore something new. Facing unfamiliar territory, uncertainty, or even potential disappointment alongside the person you care deeply for can strengthen a romantic bond by giving you the opportunity to approach the challenge as a united front. Risk-taking with your significant other is also a great way to gain insight into how you and your partner navigate the unfamiliar. There's no better way to see what someone is made of than to explore new ground together. Ultimately, a journey into the unknown with your love can bring you closer, help you gain a deeper understanding of yourselves, and confirm whether you are actually a good match for each other.

DaRealBBJudy: We were at my mother's house in New Orleans lying in bed looking at photos I had of us on my phone. We were playing around, laughing, joking, and having a great time. For every photo *Beaurtiful* and I looked at, we would banter back and forth about which one of us would post it on our social media pages first. Though she joked about posting the photos, I knew it wasn't likely that she would do it because she seldom uses social media. But I do. A lot. And since she seemed to be on board with letting the world know that she was in a relationship with me, I posted one of the photos of us together. Afterward I went to her and told her that I had done it. A look of concern came over her face, and she said, "Well, I guess I just came out then." I jokingly responded, "Should I get a cake or something?" After all those years of being closeted and private about her romantic life, our relationship was made public on my Instagram page.

Rumors had already been circulating that we were dating. We had been featured on blogs everywhere. Our unconfirmed relationship was the talk of the town in the Black social media–verse. Bloggers were having a field day trying to find out if we were truly an item. Even the paparazzi followed us around. They once caught us on the lake together and at the airport holding hands. When preparing to post the photo, I thought about what to say in the caption that would address the rumors. The only thing that came to mind was one word to confirm everything. "Yep." Yep, *Beaurtiful* is gay. Yep, she's in love with me.

Da Brat: All I could think was *Oh shit!* After more than thirty years in the closet and so much speculation, it was finally and officially out there. Nervous doesn't even begin to describe how I felt. I paced back and forth and had several drinks to try and calm myself down. Judy and I sat outside her mother's house so I could smoke and settle my nerves. We sat on the curb as I checked my social media pages to see the response. It was no surprise that my phone started blowing up. So many people were texting, calling, and commenting on Judy's post. Despite never acknowledging my sexuality in public to anyone, many people said they already knew and were offering their congratulations. There was this huge outpouring of love and support not just for me coming out but also for Judy and me as a couple.

> "U both deserve to be happy . . . congratulations 🎉👏"
> "So happy that you are happy. ❤ is in the air everywhere 🌈"
> "Congrats we love you. It's nice to see you two happy."

I really didn't expect that.

GOLDEN RULE:

"BE SUPPORTIVE."

Supportiveness is a key element of any healthy relationship, and it is especially important for couples wanting to build trust. When you and your significant other are supportive of each other, it shows that you are willing to be there for each other no matter the circumstances. This can help to create a sense of security and stability in the relationship, which is essential for trust to continue to flourish. Supportiveness can come in many ways—offering a listening ear when your partner needs one, cheering on or encouraging your loved one in their pursuit of success, or simply never failing to be by each other's side during good and bad times. As a couple, you and your partner are more likely to open up and be vulnerable with each other when you know you have unconditional support.

DaRealBBJudy: To be clear, posting the photo was not a way for me to force *Beaurtiful* out of the closet. I don't believe that you can force someone's timing anyway. I posted the photo because we both agreed that we should. Even though *Beaurtiful* wouldn't have been the one to do it for several reasons, I knew from her actions that she had become more and more comfortable with the idea of finally living her truth.

During another trip to New Orleans, we were out walking around and she grabbed my hand. Holding hands is a natural thing for couples to do. It was a mindless gesture, and I don't think *Beaurtiful* thought much of it, though she was technically still closeted. But she was feeling more assured about herself and our relationship. Her manager and security team, on the other hand, panicked. They had never seen her show PDA with anyone. They also knew her fear of public judgment about her sexuality. The minute our hands touched, her team went into crisis mode and grabbed our other hands. We were one big ole hand-holding gang walking around New Orleans because *Beaurtiful* had not shared this part of her life in public before.

I was happy that Brat wanted to take our relationship public, but after so many years of doing the same thing the same way, she didn't know how to actually live out loud. I believe this is the one thing being in a relationship with me has taught her. I've never been in the closet, but the simple gesture of her holding the hand of the person she trusts and loves in public was a huge sign that this big, scary thing that she had been fearing her entire adult life was becoming less threatening.

Da Brat: I've never been one to do public displays of affection. Every time I was with Judy, I wanted to be close to her and touch her. I would have been happy if I could get in her skin or be glued to her. I just loved being next to her. It was like the door to the closet was beginning to open for me because I had a hard time containing myself every time I was around her.

My team first learned of our relationship and our hard-to-hide attraction for each other during the 2019 Essence Festival. First of all, everyone who is anyone is always in New Orleans for the Fourth of July weekend festivities. That year Jermaine Dupri, Missy Elliott, Mary J. Blige, Nas, and Pharrell were among the list of performers. I was in town to join Jermaine and other So So Def artists onstage for a big performance to celebrate the festival's twenty-fifth anniversary. Judy accompanied me to all the rehearsals. We were getting serious, and I was caring less and less about hiding it even at this popular and well-attended event.

After finishing one of my rehearsals, Judy and I, along with my security team, went out to a restaurant. As we sat at the table waiting for our food, my security person tried to shield us from the public by holding menus up around us. While he was doing that, Judy and I were playing footsie under the table. We were likely to be seen together anyway, but I wasn't even thinking about it. Then the best, most memorable thing happened. Judy and I got up to go outside so I could have a cigarette. She grabbed my hand, and we ducked into this alleyway. Out of the blue Judy kissed me. It was our first kiss, and OMG I became like a smitten little girl all over again. I couldn't stop cheesin'.

DaRealBBJudy: By the time I posted the photo of *Beaurtiful* and me, I knew going public with our relationship was something that Brat wanted to do. While we were both having a hard time containing how attracted we were to each other, I knew for the announcement to happen that it was going to have to go through me.

I live my life unabashed and out loud. I share so much on social media. It's how I built my brand. So it made the most sense that I would be the one to post about us. I was also 99.9 percent sure that the outcome would be positive because I am an optimist. I always believe a negative can turn into a positive. I lead with expecting the best, and if the best doesn't happen, I find the best anyway.

Brat isn't wired that way. But I had tremendous confidence in the love we share and, most important, the trust we have in each other. I had no doubt that once the picture was posted and after she got through her nervousness, she would realize how much of a great thing it was going to be for her and us.

GOLDEN RULE:

"BE HONEST. OWN YOUR TRUTH."

Owning your truth is fundamental to establishing trust in a relationship. When you are able to be honest and genuine about what you think or feel with your partner, it fosters a sense of security and openness that can deepen your bond. One way to make sure honesty and truthfulness can flourish in your relationship is to maintain that, whenever you are communicating, whatever is said has a safe and supportive place to land that will not be met with a negative backlash. This means listening without judgment (even if what's being said is about something you may have done or how you make them feel) and respecting each other's right to own and articulate your feelings. It also means being willing to talk about difficult topics, even when they present a challenge to your own convictions. Another important element is making sure you and your partner consistently model honesty and truthfulness in all areas of your life. In short, your actions should definitely align with what you say. By owning your truth, you set a positive example that will encourage your partner to do the same.

Da Brat: It was such an amazing feeling to know I could be in love and not have to hide my feelings. It felt like a weight had been lifted off of me. Had I met Judy years ago, my life could have been different, but I think everything happens for a reason. I met her when I was supposed to meet her and at a time when I was ready to live my life for me and be happy. While the response to the photo was received well by everyone, it did cause some friction between my big sister Lisa Raye and me.

Several months after the photo was posted and the entire world knew that I was gay and in love with Judy, I was asked to appear on *Cocktails with Queens*, the reality TV show that Lisa Raye cohosted with three other celebrity women. Her cohosts didn't know that Lisa Raye and I had not seen each other and had not spoken in months. There wasn't bad blood between us, but I was living my life, going through some things, and not talking about any of it with her. Suddenly there was a major announcement about my life, and she knew nothing about it.

My sister and I have always been close. Even when I was closeted I would make sure to introduce her to damn near every one of my girlfriends *and* boyfriends. As my big sister she shielded me and my relationships. Her issue with my coming out was that I didn't share any of it with her. She learned the news just like the rest of the world did—through social media.

I love Lisa Raye very much and never intended to make her feel slighted, but I was on some grown-woman shit at the time. I was trying to deal with everything on my own, and I just didn't feel like talking about it with her or anyone. I didn't want my decisions to be judged, and I also didn't want to hear anyone's fucking opinions about my choices, my partner, and my life.

My relationship with Judy was my special secret that I wanted to keep until I was ready to share it. I wanted to protect it like I had to protect everything else my entire life. So until Judy and I were solid, I opted not to tell anyone about us, including my sister. I know it hurt her and she felt left out, but it was what I needed to do and how I wanted to handle it.

The response to my "coming out announcement photo" was better than I could ever have imagined. I believe it worked out so well because I have never felt as safe with anyone as I do with Judy. Her love and instincts allowed me to trust that whatever happened after deciding to own my truth, I wasn't going to face it alone. Judy opened the door for me to come out, but she would have never done it had we not decided together to let the world know. But, also, if we had not built our relationship on love, unwavering support, and trust.

The Takeaway

As an LGBTQIA+ couple that began with a celebrity partner in the closet, more than anything we wanted to live our life openly like other individuals in romantic relationships. Until a decision was made to take our partnership public, we chose to direct our energies toward building a relationship grounded in love, respect, and trust so we could continue to thrive in spite of an often invasive public. Fostering trust in our relationship and placing trustworthy people around us made all the difference in enabling our relationship to grow in private. Without trust we would have never been able to comfortably share ourselves with each other and our life with the public. Here are some of the golden rules we live by that continue to help our relationship blossom:

1. **Set firm boundaries.** If social media and living unabashedly are major parts of your partner's life like they are in ours, it should be expected that your significant other will want to share every detail, which may include you. So talk to them and set some guidelines about what is and isn't okay to share—not just on social media but in general. Before the picture "announcement" was posted, the both of us refrained from sharing anything about our relationship. The rules were that it was private. Even as the blogs speculated, we didn't confirm or deny. Neither of us had to worry about the other responding on behalf of the relationship. We were committed to trusting each other.

Breaking the rules is a guaranteed way to breach trust. So don't do it. If you feel the rules need to be amended, then talk to your partner about your concerns, ideas, plans, and desires first *before* doing anything that you haven't agreed to.

2. **Trust is earned.** When you're dating, observe how your partner behaves when there are no rules. Does their character line up with what you're looking for? Are you comfortable with how they engage whether in private or in public? Are they loose with the lips about things happening in your life, their life, or others' lives? Keep a watchful eye on how your partner moves. Shady boots come in all sizes—straight, gay, male, female, trans—and must be avoided, otherwise all your shit will be in the streets, chile. FYI . . . trust can't be forced. But it is damn sure earned.

3. **Read the tea leaves.** Despite Brat's being closeted and our relationship being on private status, it was Brat who was becoming increasingly more comfortable with public displays of affection. As we lay in the bed in New Orleans laughing about posting pictures of us on Instagram, it was clear that she was getting to a place where going public would become a reality. In the beginning we were to keep things mum, but as our feelings for each other progressed, Brat was the one who would initiate PDA like holding hands in public. Had there been signs that she was still uncomfortable, that picture of us would never have been posted. It's ideal if your partner is supercommunicative and speaks their mind to you about everything. For those who are less talkative, be mindful of nonverbal cues that signify what they're feeling. Is that

loud sigh an indication that they don't like something you said or did? Do they roll their eyes when you mention a particular person? We're not suggesting that you become a mind reader, but we are recommending that you pay attention. Your relationship will be better off because it will show your partner that you are present and taking heed of what they communicate verbally or otherwise.

4. **Trust your gut.** Your gut feelings are an amazing heads-up for when something may be awry in your relationship or if you're feeling doubtful about the trustworthiness of your partner. Whether it's your gut or a tiny voice in your head that says something or someone isn't on the up-and-up, believe it. Our instincts are knowledgeable and valuable. Sometimes we don't want to listen to what we inherently know to be true so we wait for something big to happen as proof that "Yep, I knew that good-for-nothing individual wasn't telling the truth." Instead of waiting for the big thing, pay attention to the small things and let your inner voice be your guide.

5. **Be ready for war.** If your goal is to build a relationship that lasts, you have to be ready to battle with (and sometimes for) your partner at any given time. No one wants to be in a relationship and have to stand alone. In the J+B relationship dictionary, *trust* means to be down for whatever, whenever, for the one you love. While one of us formally came out with the posting of the photo, we were without a doubt a united front. Luckily, the overall response to the news was favorable. But we were ready to do battle together with anyone who dared to bring the negative.

Reflection

Da Brat

My mom and dad were never together so I didn't grow up in a traditional type of home. I lived with my mother and grandmother and frequently visited my dad's side of the family. I enjoyed spending time with Dad's family. They always spoiled me. My paternal grandfather was a chef. I don't remember what my grandmother did. But she was amazing. Unlike my mother's family, I wasn't the only grandchild on my father's side. My cousins and I could go outside and stay out all night if we wanted to because everybody knew one another on the block. My dad's family always let me run free. I got to be a tomboy over there. I got to wild out, ride my bike, pop wheelies, and play with bugs. When I returned to the home I shared with my mother and superreligious granny, I had to go back to being a girly girl who wore dresses and was a prim and proper lady. It really was the best of both worlds.

5 Respect

Marriage, dating, and partnership are much more fun when, in addition to the love, you're with someone you respect. It is possible to be in a relationship with a person you respect but don't love, but it is hard as hell to be with someone you love but don't respect.

How is that even possible? Don't love and respect intersect? Our answer is yes *and* no.

From our standpoint, it depends on how you personally define love. For example, respect may be a major value for you in romantic relationships. You may desire someone (or someones, because monogamy isn't the only way people engage in relationships) who doesn't just say they love you but shows it by respecting who you are—your feelings, opinions, experience, and shit, even your motherfucking time. *C'mon, somebody!* So in that case, love and respect do intersect because what you require is a 360-type of situation—a love where you and your partner are not only willing but also capable of sustaining a partnership where you each feel seen, heard, valued, and completely loved.

On the other hand, there are plenty of people who are in relationships with someone they love or say they love but do not respect. Take for instance a relationship where there is cheating. Cheating ain't nothing but 100 percent unfiltered disrespect. If you're in a monogamous relationship and your partner seeks romantic intimacy with someone else, respect for the other person and the sanctity of the relationship has for damn sure exited the chat. We know this because we've both been cheaters in prior relationships. While there was once love in those situations where we stepped out on our former partners, the experience taught us both valuable lessons about the importance of communication, consideration, and respect.

Fortunately, the love between us is very strong. It's largely due to us being intentional about being good to each other, loyal, supportive, and considerate. But we're not infallible. There are times we have to remind each other to be mindful of the other's feelings and decisions. Although we always find a way to work through things, the one area that always seems to trip us up is our reality show, *Brat Loves Judy.*

GOLDEN RULE:

"SUPPORT EACH OTHER'S DECISIONS."

Supporting your partner's choices is essential for cultivating respect and establishing a solid foundation of trust and understanding.

When you show that you are prepared to stick by your boo and accept their decisions, you demonstrate your dedication to their happiness and well-being. By supporting your partner's choices, it demonstrates that you respect their perspectives, thoughts, and emotions. It also signals that you have the utmost confidence in their judgment. Trusting your partner's decision-making sends a message that you have faith in their abilities and feel they can make excellent decisions that will be beneficial for the both of you.

Da Brat: It seems like we argue the most when we are filming the show. While some shows are scripted, ours isn't. The things that happen on the show are actually things that happen in our day-to-day lives.

The show's episodes are built off what we've got going on in our lives. There may be something going on with our son or an issue happening with Kaleidoscope, I'm working on something music-related, or we're planning to attend the BET awards or something like that. The production team for our show is there to shoot the interactions between us and the people in our camp.

A disagreement between Judy and me usually happens when the production team asks us to do something that I don't want to do. They may want us to talk about our child or rehash an argument that we had that we've already resolved. If we've patched things up, I don't want to bring the issue up again. I feel it's better for us and our relationship to just move on. Besides, the cameras don't need all of that and neither do we as a couple.

But production will say, "We'd really like for you to talk about that subject some more." I'll refuse, but Judy will want us to deal with the issue and recommend that we get some kind of closure. She believes if the production team captured us arguing about something and we resolved things off camera, then we need to tie up loose ends and show how we worked things out for our audience.

Although we are committed to doing a reality show about our relationship and enjoy giving our fans glimpses into our life together, there are some things I don't want to be recorded for the show. I've always been private, and though I am living out loud and detailing so much of my life for the show, if I tell the production team, "No, I don't think it's a good idea" or "I just don't want to do it," that should be the end of it. Most of the time it's not because Judy will intervene.

Judy will go talk to the producers then come to me and suggest we do what I have already said no to but in a way that feels right to us. Every time that happens I get frustrated because it makes me feel like she's taking someone else's side against me and my feelings are being disregarded. If I say I don't want to do something that should be the be-all and end-all. We shouldn't have to have a conversation about how to get it done when I've already indicated that I don't want to do it.

DaRealBBJudy: My two cents is that my wife always thinks I am taking someone else's side and not respecting her wishes when it comes to issues about the show, but we aren't just cast, we're also executive producers. I'm never going to take someone else's side over my wife's, but I am able to see opportunities in situations that my wife may not. *Beaurtiful* has been a performer her whole life. That's an area she knows extremely well. I am naturally a content creator. It's what I do well.

If there's something that *Beaurtiful* says no to for the show, I usually know why. I will have a conversation with the producers to hear their perspective and then go back to my wife to discuss how we can capture the moment but in a way that feels right to us. I'll go to her and say, "Let's do it this way." My goal is to always figure out how to be truthful and respectful of our relationship, our family, *and* her feelings. She may not want to film certain things, but if the idea is good for the show and truthfully depicts how we communicate and resolve conflicts in our relationship, I believe we should do it but in *our* way.

Da Brat: I understand what my wife wants to do, but I often feel the production team knows how to get what they want and it's by using her. I have no doubt that they're like, "If Brat says no, let's go around her and ask Judy."

I believe they do that because they know Judy will try to figure it out, and what happens is we end up doing the thing the production team wanted—the thing I had said no to in the beginning. That shit pisses me off because it makes me feel like no one—my wife in particular—is listening to me. If I say no to something for the show, the production team should not be talking with Judy so she can get me to do it. It's their job to come up with some other ideas. My wife may not think she's taking their side, but that's what it feels like to me. In my opinion, the way respect works in a relationship is that before you make a decision you should always think of your partner, especially if it is something you know they may not like or it's something they disapprove of.

GOLDEN RULE:

"LISTEN TO EACH OTHER."

Listening is a sign of respect in a relationship because it shows that you value what your significant other has to say. When you listen attentively, you are making an effort to understand their point of view and to see things from their perspective. This can help to build a stronger connection between you and your partner, as well as foster a more respectful and understanding relationship. Listening involves more than just hearing the words that your partner says. It is also about understanding what the words they're saying actually mean so you can act upon them if and/or when needed. In addition to showing respect, listening can help to resolve conflict in a relationship. When you understand what your significant other has shared about their wants, needs, or concerns, you are able to be a better and more supportive partner who's able to find solutions to problems that will be mutually beneficial to the relationship. If you want to build a healthy and respectful relationship, then listening is one of the most important things you can do. By listening to your partner, you are showing them that you care about them, that you are interested in understanding them, and that you want to build a strong and lasting relationship with them.

DaRealBBJudy: I feel that in relationships respect is definitely directly connected to consideration. Since we are making a show together, I feel like there should be some discussion about ideas instead of just saying, "No, we ain't doing it." My objective is to always make a great piece of content, and if there's something *Beaurtiful* doesn't want to do, I think we should have a conversation about it before she just opts out. Most of the time I will be the one to sit in on the planning sessions with the staff. What I don't think *Beaurtiful* is aware of is that some of those ideas the production team asks us to do may have originally come from me.

In season one of *Brat Loves Judy*, *Beaurtiful* didn't want to argue in front of the cameras. She wanted the camera crew to stop shooting if we were in a disagreement. I told her that we should be authentic and let the argument happen so the audience can see the whole thing—from argument to resolution. That was a primary reason why we decided to do this reality show in the first place. We wanted to give the public access to our lives so they could see that as an LGBTQIA+ couple, our relationship and marriage is no different than anyone else's. We love, disagree, and live our lives just like any other couple.

Our differing viewpoints on what should and should not be done for the show is an ongoing struggle. *Beaurtiful* is often adamant about not doing certain things, and I believe some of her unwillingness comes from the place where she's thinking ahead. She admits to being suspicious and looking for ulterior motives in everyone. With the show, she tries to figure out what the production team is doing and how they're trying to make her look instead of thinking about how they may be attempting to piece things together.

She's been doing television far longer than I have. It's not lost on me the concern she has about how she may be portrayed. In social media, they say things go down in the DMs. In reality TV, things go down in the editing bay. So I do understand her concerns. But if we need to shoot a specific scene because it connects to something I shot earlier that she may not know about, while she might not want to do it, the need to connect the pieces is still there.

I'll try to work with the production team to find a way to get things done. My decision to do so is not out of spite or disregard for *Beaurtiful*'s feelings. There are some scenes that are needed. I prefer she and I discuss how to get it done so it is reflective of who we naturally are and how we interact—and not what the production team believes would make good television.

Da Brat: My bottom line is, if I say I don't want to do something for the show, that should be it. There shouldn't be any "let's work it out or reframe the idea" . . . nothing. I say let the production team figure something else out because if I say I don't like it, or don't want to do it because it makes me feel some type of way, that's how I feel. Any attempt to find a work-around after I have said no makes me look like what I say doesn't fucking matter and that's just not cool.

DaRealBBJudy: How we handle certain issues on the show is a part of our relationship that we continue to work on. It's because we respect each other so much that we keep trying. Eventually we will find a compromise, or not. One thing is for certain: We are steadfast about being respectful and considerate of each other. Disrespect doesn't happen much in our relationship. But there was one time when the shoe was on the other foot, and I was the one who was frustrated.

A few years ago *Beaurtiful* did an interview on her friend's YouTube show. During this interview she talked about some sexual stuff with an ex, and the video went viral! Prior to the whole internet hearing about her sexual exploits with a former partner, I was already in my feelings. I didn't like that she talked about it because she wouldn't want me to tell people about how I did what I did with any of my exes. I know she didn't mean any harm. She was just doing an interview, answering questions, and not thinking. We worked through the situation together, but the issue didn't go away.

Every time someone posted about the video interview, it was "Da Brat, who is the girlfriend of or now married to . . ." I hated that I was attached to this fucking video conversation. I also hated that the video had gone viral and I had to see it on every platform. It was bad enough that *Beaurtiful* talked about the things she used to do with her ex, but it was made worse because I was also dragged into the conversation because we are a couple.

GOLDEN RULE:

"TAKE RESPONSIBILITY."

Showing accountability is the ultimate sign of respect because it indicates that you understand the impact your words and actions can have on the relationship. Taking responsibility means you are willing to own up to your mistakes and take the necessary steps to fix them. Being able to take responsibility is a way to show your partner that being in a stable, mature, responsible relationship is important to you. It also shows how you're willing to take responsible actions in order to overcome a potential challenge to the relationship. When you take responsibility in a relationship, you are not only showing your partner that you respect them, but you are also letting them know that you have a strong sense of self-worth and integrity as well. Taking responsibility isn't easy, but it is an important step in being able to build and maintain a healthy relationship.

Da Brat: I had no idea Judy was gonna feel disrespected by that conversation. Had I known, I would not have said what I did. After the video came out, Judy didn't seem to be too bothered by the racy conversation. She mentioned it to me a few times, but I never got the sense that she was angry. I believe it was after the video interview gained traction that she got frustrated. She complained about all the Google alerts mentioning her name in association with the video, and the shit was getting on her nerves. Judy asked me if I would have liked it if the roles were reversed. She wanted to know if she had been the one to discuss the things she used to do for a former partner, would I be comfortable hearing about it every day? Of course my answer was no, I wouldn't have liked it. But the reality was I did an interview with a friend I have known for a long time, got too comfortable, and dove in a little too deep about something that should have stayed private.

We may upset each other at times and not see eye to eye on everything, but my wife and I work hard at maintaining the levels of respect in our relationship. Say what you will about us, but we are very loyal to each other. A few years ago Judy and I invited some friends and family members over to our house to hang out. Someone who had been a friend of Judy's had a little too much to drink, and her behavior toward Judy went from friendly to very inappropriate. At one point they even suggested that I go upstairs to bed because I "looked tired." My good friends who were watching the situation play out pulled me to the side and said I needed to keep an eye on this person because something wasn't right about them. As the saying goes, when alcohol goes in, the truth comes out. It became obvious to me that Judy's friend had been crushing on her for some time and too much alcohol put those feelings on blast.

I kept an eye on Judy's friend who continued with their inappropriate behavior. I opted not to make a scene so I wouldn't embarrass my wife. Later on I suggested that she cut ties with this person because they wanted more than just friendship. Judy and I ride for each other no matter what. She made no excuses for her friend. She took action and cut that person off immediately.

DaRealBBJudy: I had no problem ending the friendship because I can't ask Brat to do something that I wouldn't be willing to do myself. It would be fucked up for me to cut up and throw a phone across the room about "pretty toes" and then act like my former friend's inappropriate behavior with me wasn't a problem as well.

The Takeaway

One of the goals for our relationship from the get-go has been to make sure that respect and love are always the norm. If or when something difficult happens—we disagree, we fight, whatever it is—we choose to work our way back to that place of respect and love quickly. This choice to resolve our struggles immediately is due to a mutual understanding that in order for us to maintain a healthy relationship, respect for each other is critical. We don't just require respect from each other, we also require others to respect us as a couple and as individuals. To put it simply—we don't play about each other. As some people and social media trolls have learned, if you say something snide to us or do something disrespectful, you will get dealt with. We work hard to hold each other and those who come into our lives accountable because this union of ours means a lot to us. Here are some additional golden rules that can help you and your significant other maintain respect in your relationship:

1. **Keep the lines of communication open.** A steady flow of conversation keeps us feeling connected. Sharing the details of our days and knowing what went down in our friendships and work lives bonds us together even when our schedules try to keep us apart.

2. **Understand your partner's dos and don'ts.** If you know there are things that grind your partner's gears, for the sake of the relationship—don't do them. In the alternative, if there are

things that make them happy, by all means you should make them happen. They'll appreciate your consideration in both instances.

3. **Find the compromise.** Though Brat may be headstrong about what we shoot for the reality show, we do try to find a compromise that addresses both of our concerns. Sometimes after we have had a private discussion about what is needed and why it is important, we'll decide how to proceed together. Most of the time the resolution is shooting scenes in a manner that feels good to both of us. During those rare times when we're not able to find a compromise, we refrain from pressuring each other to do things we are adamant about not doing.

4. **Be loyal.** In the words of Kendrick Lamar, "all we got is us," so put that woman (or man) first. It should also go without saying, but the best way to show you are loyal to your partner is to not cheat. Cheating is the ultimate disrespect. If your feelings for your partner have gone south and you no longer wish to be in the relationship, find the exit. Ending the relationship will always be the better decision than breaking a promise to be faithful.

5. **Show some love.** Take an interest in what interests your partner. There's no better way to shower respect on the one you love than to engage in the things they love. If you want your partner to feel seen and valued, join them in their favorite activity or engage them in conversation about something they like.

DaRealBBJudy: Our pillow-talk game is top notch. It's our time to connect and we lie there and talk like girlfriends. Our conversations run the gamut. They can be about something happening with my business, a hairstyle I am about to have done, and more. I appreciate that *Beaurtiful* always wants to know what is going on in my world.

6 Sexual Chemistry

There's no other way to say it. Forever with someone that you don't want to get your freak on with will be a long-ass time. But not every relationship needs to have an intense sexual connection. We consider ourselves lucky that on top of all the great things we provide for each other, great sex is also on the list. Whether we would turn out to be fantastic partners in life and in the bedroom wasn't apparent when we first met. But the more we got to know each other, the sparks between us intensified and unmasked a sexual chemistry neither of us had ever experienced with any other person.

GOLDEN RULE:

"BE OPEN TO LOVE."

Your tough outer shell is there to keep the creepy folks away, but if you want one of those heart-fluttering romances to come into your life, you're gonna have to let your vulnerable side show more. That means opening not just your heart but your mind to love. If you want to experience love, you have to believe not only that it's possible for you, but also that you're deserving of it. Another thing you'll need to open is your mouth. So communicate. Share your honest thoughts. Be transparent about what you like. Take a chance and say something you've been holding back or were afraid to share. Vulnerability is never easy. No one wants to express something personal only to feel judged or have their feelings disregarded. But love is a risk. Just as you want to get to know a prospective partner, they also want to get to know you. Share the things that you feel, what you love to do, or what makes you the baddest bitch or butch when you walk into a room. Being open to love will also require a willingness to compromise, listen, and work with your partner to build a strong and healthy relationship. Embracing love means you're ready to put your whole self out there so you can experience something beautiful and transformative with someone special who has captured your eye and hopefully your heart.

Da Brat: The attraction to my wife and our subsequent relationship and marriage really caught me by surprise. The day we met in person for the first time and when she came to visit me at the recording studio might be all the proof anyone needs that your destiny will meet up with you when it's meant to happen. I wasn't just thrown off by how direct Judy was about her interest in me, my response also had me taken aback.

Normally I am the coolest motherfucker ever. But not that day. She had me stumbling and fumbling. It had a lot to do with the fact that Judy is very attractive. She's just so damn pretty. I could always tell when other people were interested in me. But Judy hit me with the whammy. I didn't know she was into women, and I for damn sure didn't have a clue that she would want to date a celebrity rapper. My persona is that I'm the kind of person who will fuck somebody up, shoot 'em bang-bang. And here she is, this successful entrepreneur and inspirational speaker, telling me she was interested in me. Surprise . . . surprise!

As I got to know Judy more, I discovered her heart is just as beautiful as her appearance. I got butterflies the first time we met, and they have never gone away. It's how she looks at me. It makes me feel so special. Our conversations also grab me. She intrigued me from the very beginning. As our relationship grew, I realized I was a goner and had fallen deeply in love with her and hated whenever we were apart. I tell people all the time that I've never in my life felt this kind of connection with anyone.

Whenever I was around Judy, I would get these weird pains and have funny feelings in my chest. My knees would weaken and my nerves would get shaky. In my head I'd be thinking, *What the fuck is going on? I never get nervous! I am Da Brat!* I can get on the stage before crowds of people and rock the mic. I can do anything.

I have balls of steel. I will cuss any motherfucker out, disrespect anybody, shoot anybody. But Judy somehow wipes all of that machisma away. For so long, I've had this invisible coat of armor around myself, and here comes Judy wiping it away by being herself.

During the beginning stages of our relationship, it seemed like every time Judy and I were together I would revert to acting like a little girl with a massive crush. Judy would be trying to have a conversation with me, and as she's talking I'm trying to hide my face from her. I'd sit on the side of her or behind her so she couldn't look at me directly. When I wasn't playing this odd game of adult peekaboo, I'd regularly check the corners of my mouth to make sure there wasn't anything there. I would obsessively put Carmex on my lips so they wouldn't look dry. I can only imagine what Judy was thinking about my quirky behavior, but my insecurities were having a field day.

Growing up, I was an incredibly shy child. I thought I was an ugly duckling. I would refuse to smile because I thought my teeth were too big for my mouth. Whenever I talked or smiled I would put my hand over my lips in order to cover up my big Bugs Bunny teeth. I came into my own as a young woman. Can't be a hip-hop star and not have an insane amount of confidence. But all that shit went right out the window when Judy came into the picture. Here I am—this grown-ass woman who has lived a lot of life—and I'm nervous. I'm attracted to a beautiful woman and praying she doesn't notice any imperfections so she doesn't question whether she likes me as much as she thought she did. When I was alone I would look at myself in the mirror and say, "Bitch, who the fuck *are* you? Pull yourself together!" Each time I would be in Judy's presence, my feelings would once again have me bouncing off the walls.

GOLDEN RULE:

"GO AFTER WHAT YOU WANT."

You don't have to be confident to act confidently. Confidence is reinforced by action. So go after that person who makes your body feel all tingly when they're around. Asserting yourself shows that you are willing to take risks and put yourself out there, which can be very attractive to potential romantic partners. When you actively pursue your desires, you are showing that you value yourself and your needs. This assertiveness can be a powerful magnet for those who are genuinely compatible with you, as they will be drawn to your authenticity and vulnerability. Be clear about what you are looking for in a partner and why you're interested in them. Rejection is sadly a natural part of the journey, so try not to let it deter you from showing that you're ready for love. Just don't spend any unnecessary time chasing someone who has made it clear they're not the one for you. Do yourself a favor and keep it moving. By being authentic and true to yourself, you'll eventually find someone who genuinely appreciates and values you for who you are. And if you don't, that's okay, too. As the song goes, "Don't push it. Don't force it. Let it happen naturally."

DaRealBBJudy: I was immediately attracted to my *Beaurtiful.* It's hard not to be. She's gorgeous. But her physical appearance isn't the only thing that makes her attractive. Sexual chemistry isn't just about looks, it's about how the person makes you feel. What made me make the first move and express my interest in getting to know her is how warm and inviting she is. She's totally real and very nurturing. It's like her emotions will completely embrace you. It's probably why she gives the best hugs. She's such a beautiful person. When we were initially getting to know each other, I was so surprised by how different she is from her rap persona. There's this tough exterior, but underneath it is this sweet and really shy woman. Often, at the start of our relationship, I was the one who would initiate anything romantic. We liked each other a lot, but she wouldn't make the first move. Everything changed during the 2019 Essence Festival, when my *Beaurtiful* had come to New Orleans to perform. As shy as she had been around me previously, neither of us could contain how immensely attracted we were to each other.

Da Brat: There was this one moment while I was rehearsing for So So Def's Essence Festival performance that I have never forgotten. Judy had to use the bathroom. I got up to show her where it was. She was inside the bathroom for a while, but I didn't want to leave her. I stood outside the door and waited for her like a goofy. When she came out of the bathroom, we moved in toward each other for an embrace. We stood there outside the bathroom just holding each other. My insides melted. I didn't want to let her go. The hug was everything. She says I give good hugs, but she gives good hugs, too! We finally pulled away from each other, and my body was tingling all over.

GOLDEN RULE:

"GET YOUR FLIRT ON."

Flirting with someone you are interested in is an enjoyable and exciting way to connect and can also lay the groundwork for a meaningful love connection. However, it is important to remember to keep things lighthearted and playful and to always respect a person's boundaries. The purpose of flirting is to test the waters to see if there is a spark of chemistry between you and your potential sweetheart. It allows you to showcase your charm and wit while gauging their interest with the hope that a romantic relationship will blossom. But you don't have to be looking for love to flirt. If you're already in a relationship, flirting with your significant other is a great way to keep the fire between you lit, as it signals to your partner that you are still attracted to and enjoy being with them. A little playful banter can also add some sexual energy if things have gotten somewhat stale. Just don't start flirting with other people unless that's permissible in your relationship. So, don't be afraid to flirt a little bit and see where it leads. You could find yourself on the path to a new romance or reignite the passion with your current love.

DaRealBBJudy: July 1 is the date that we have determined is the official start of our relationship because that was the day that we hugged. Our first kiss happened later in that alleyway outside of a restaurant. I made the first move again. I remember later that night she asked me if I was gonna stay with her at her hotel. I said, "Oh no! I'm not sleeping here." Another thing that I found so endearing about *Beaurtiful* is that she's not intrusive. She's very much the type to follow my lead and take her time. When I told her I wasn't going to stay in the hotel with her, she responded that she wasn't going to do anything to me. I looked at her and said, "How do you know I wasn't going to try and do something to you?"

Beaurtiful didn't make any moves early on. We laugh about it now because sex is an important part of our marriage. But back then, she wanted me to know that she was a gentle lady. I made sure not to stay at her hotel with her that night because I'm *not* a gentle lady. The first time we spent a night together was during one of my trips to Atlanta. She left me in the bed and went to sleep on the sofa because she felt like she needed to give me space. I got up and followed her ass to the sofa.

Despite having intense sexual chemistry, we waited to have sex. Living in different cities had a lot to do with it, and, of course, *Beaurtiful*'s shyness. I was ready for us to do it. I was nervous but felt like it was time. We slept beside each other so many times without doing anything. We'd play and roll around but stop at the next step. I was doing my best to entice her. Whenever we were together I would put on these pretty matching bra-and-panty sets. At one point *Beaurtiful* said to me, "You just walk around the house with no clothes on?" My response was, "Am I not supposed to?"

GOLDEN RULE:

"SAVOR THE SLOW BURN."

Sexual tension adds excitement and anticipation to a relationship, making spending time together a priority. It's a lot like having an itch that no matter how much you try to ignore it, will only feel better once it's scratched. A relationship charged with sexual tension can also help you and your partner connect on a deeper level, both emotionally and physically. This heightened sense of longing can lead to more meaningful conversations and a greater willingness to explore and understand each other's needs. While sexual tension in a relationship can be nerve-racking, keep in mind that this constant feeling of desire is the goal. You should want to be with your partner, and those feelings should be reciprocated. By embracing and harnessing the tension that you feel, you and your significant other can cultivate a passionate, fulfilling connection that's built on mutual affection that energizes the relationship every time you're together.

Da Brat: There was this one time we were together in Atlanta. We had not had sex yet. We were still sleeping in the same bed but had not done the damn thing. Judy had gotten up to go to the bathroom. She had on these thong panties, and I watched her as she made her way to the bathroom. Her ass was wiggling all over the place. I had never seen anything like it. It was like her booty had its own rhythm. I thought to myself, *Now, how the fuck am I gonna be able to handle all of that?* I was mesmerized. It's one thing to see that ass in her clothes. It's another thing to see it in a thong. I remember thinking that when we finally had sex, I had to make sure I was good.

DaRealBBJudy: What makes our sex life so wonderful is that we both have giving personalities, and that shows up in the bedroom. We enjoy being able to pleasure each other. It's who we are. *Beaurtiful* has a big heart and so do I. We are happiest when we are able to make each other happy inside and outside of the bedroom. We are also respectful of each other's space. We are mindful of our body language and take cues from each other before and during sex.

If I had to choose, I'd say between the two of us, *Beaurtiful* has the stronger sex drive. She was shy and apprehensive about having sex with me when we first got together, but she's not that way anymore. Now she has no problem initiating it. While we both enjoy giving to each other in the bedroom, *Beaurtiful*'s preference is to focus on me. One time she made me orgasm eleven times! The next day I was fucked up. I couldn't get out of bed and walk straight. Multiple orgasms take all of the energy out of me. I needed to rest for the day! I always want *Beaurtiful* to have the same experience, but she refuses to let me reciprocate in that way. There's a certain tolerance you have to build up to be able to sustain double-digit orgasms. She'll let me bring her to orgasm once, and then that's it. But with me she'll keep going as long as I'm willing. She'll aim for at least two orgasms, but if I don't tell her to stop she'll keep going. I tell her all the time it can't just be me and she should let me have my turn to make her go crazy, but she won't let me.

GOLDEN RULE:

"SEXUAL INTIMACY MUST BE A PRIORITY."

Sexual intimacy is a necessary aspect of a healthy and fulfilling relationship. Regular physical intimacy fosters emotional closeness and strengthens your bond. Making time for sexual intimacy not only brings pleasure and physical satisfaction to a relationship, but it also enhances communication and connection. Intimate moments in the bedroom provide an opportunity for you and your partner to openly and honestly express and fulfill your desires, needs, and preferences. Failing to nurture this aspect of your relationship may lead to discontent and a desire to find fulfillment elsewhere. While it's not a guarantee, a relationship where sexual intimacy is prioritized helps lay the groundwork for a long-lasting, loving partnership. The mutual understanding and openness that's cultivated in the bedroom can spill over into other aspects of the relationship. By making sexual intimacy an essential part of your relationship, you and your partner will be able to maintain a strong sense of closeness and create a more fulfilling partnership centered on both physical and emotional connection.

Da Brat: I just love being intimate with my wife. I love the way she looks at me. I love the way she kisses me. She's just so beautiful and very sexy. Each time I look at Judy, I feel like I could just eat her up like she was a snack. I often look at her and stare in awe because I can't believe she's mine. And most of the time I just want to rip her clothes off. I don't mind being the one to give her pleasure when we're being intimate because I really enjoy watching her orgasm. It's like the best thing ever. I never want to stop because I know it makes her feel so good, and that's why I keep going and going. I will give her a few minutes to take a break, but I continue to pleasure her because I am turned on by her being turned on.

DaRealBBJudy: There are many things I enjoy about intimacy with *Beaurtiful*. What I love the most is how she doesn't hold back. When she's feeling stuff I'll automatically know it because she is so expressive. She will make all kinds of noises, or I will be able to see it with how her body is moving. Our sexual connection is intense because we love being with each other, but we also spent time learning what we both like before we were actually intimate so when we finally got down to doing it, it was (and continues to be) enjoyable for us both.

The Takeaway

Sexual chemistry is an important aspect of a relationship, but it isn't everything. We're very fortunate that our love story includes a strong sexual connection that we've successfully maintained from the honeymoon phase to marriage. Keeping the fire lit in the bedroom can be a difficult task as you learn more about and grow with your partner. Here are some additional golden rules that help keep the sexual chemistry between us intact even as our personal and professional lives evolve:

1. **Get physical.** Don't hesitate to reach out and touch your partner. Slap that booty every now and again. Grab their hand when they least expect it. Make physical touch a staple in how you engage with each other. Before we took the plunge and got intimate, we would sleep together in the same bed without doing anything. We just like to be close to each other. We also enjoyed doing simple things like holding hands, hugging, sneaking kisses, and roughhousing in the bedroom. Physical touch is an easy way to let your partner know you desire them.

2. **Ask for feedback.** After our first sexual endeavor we talked about what we each liked and wanted more (or less) of during the act. We asked each other how things felt and whether something we did should be done differently to make the experience more pleasurable. Getting feedback on your lovemaking sessions will help you learn about your partner's desires. You may have a bunch of fancy tricks in your arsenal that have worked well on other people, but your partner may hate them. Asking for feedback provides you with a road map to make sure pleasure and satisfaction are the final outcomes of your intimate moments.

3. **Don't be selfish.** Climaxing with your partner should be like Oprah's old giveaways—*Everybody gets to have an orgasm!* If you or your partner is only worried about your own satisfaction, your sex life will eventually hit the skids. You have to make sure there's balance and you give just as much as you receive.

4. **Determine the rules of engagement.** Before asking for feedback, make sure you are consistently having a conversation about what is and is not allowable during intimacy. If you are interested in trying something new, be sure to discuss it with your partner beforehand. If you try something that you didn't clear with them ahead of time, if they say stop, then it's game over. All activity should cease immediately. Even as a married couple we talk to each other all the time about consent. Whether you are in a new relationship or you've been with your partner for quite some time, we recommend you check in with each other to determine what your sexual rules of engagement are at all times.

Reflection

DaRealBBJudy

When I was super young I used to play in my father's hair. There's a picture of us where he's lying on his stomach and I'm sitting across his back and I have a million barrettes on his head. My parents sent me to private school because they wanted me to be a doctor or lawyer. None of that was what I wanted to do.

I liked doing hair. I would do hair to make money. It's just something I had a passion for. At the age of fifteen I got pregnant with my daughter, my first child. I then got pregnant again and had a son. My third pregnancy was with a set of twins (which I later miscarried). My mother put me out the house when she learned I was pregnant again. One of my friends, who was also a hair client, called my parents and told them. My mom said she put me out the house because I was being too rebellious. I decided to move in with my baby daddy. That situation was a total shit show. We would argue and fight all the time. I used to call my daddy to complain because he was always my protector.

7 Leading/Following

One of the rules we set in our relationship when we decided that we were going to be in this love thing with each other for the rest of our lives was that there would be no HBIC, or head bitch in charge. That may not sound believable when you have two high-profile women with a laundry list of accomplishments between us, but it's true. While many couples jockey for position to be on top literally and figuratively, we allow each other to lead in the areas where we are most strong.

GOLDEN RULE:

"SET THE HOUSE RULES."

Establishing roles and setting boundaries in a relationship will be important if you'd like to keep the peace. By setting some rules, you and your partner can make it easier to streamline how the relationship functions. The rules you create should outline your communication style, decision-making processes, and how you will handle things when shit hits the fan. Setting rules can also prevent conflicts and misunderstandings from becoming ugly power struggles where you're both vying to sit in the driver's seat. Your rules should become your relationship's guidebook that serves as a reminder to collaborate and compromise. Your house rules should also address accountability and responsibility, as this allows you and your partner to tailor your roles to accommodate your individual strengths and preferences. Rules don't have to be tools that stifle the natural flow in a relationship, but they are helpful in outlining what you expect from and how you will engage with each other.

DaRealBBJudy: As a first generation multimillionaire, I have taken on the role of being a caretaker for everyone in my life. I am the one my family (and friends) know they can lean on because I am a giver, a resource, and a problem solver. If there's a crisis, or an unexpected debt, everyone calls on Judy. I never had a problem with taking on the responsibility of being the one who is reliable and gets shit done because it comes naturally to me. I also believe if you are in the position to help others, then you should.

Like most Black women who put everything and everyone on their back, I have never had anyone actually take care of me until my wife. She came into my life and immediately made me and my happiness her priority. It's actually taken me some time to get used to it because I like doing shit myself. I like handling all the things. It wasn't until I learned to be okay with letting some things go that I got to experience the joy of having someone take the lead on things so I didn't have to. And, because we understand what each other's strengths are, it has been easy for us to divvy up responsibilities according to what we know or do best.

I have always been anal about budgeting and bill paying. I primarily handle the management of our money. *Beaurtiful* manages all aspects of keeping our house in order. She handles everything from scheduling the landscaping team to hiring people to wash our cars and clean our pool and more. Because we're both leading in the areas where we are the strongest, there are no arguments or fussing with each other about these things. If there's an issue or question or anything that comes up that has to do with money, she will quite often leave it up to me. If someone wants to know where something is for the house or when something was last fixed or if we actually need to have something fixed, I refer them to *Beaurtiful.*

Da Brat: A big mistake any couple can make is thinking that your husband, wife, lover, partner is someone you need to control. I am thankful that my wife and I believe so strongly in partnership and allowing each other to seek fulfillment in the things that we naturally excel in. But we're also comfortable with who we are as women and with stepping back and allowing the other to take the reins not because we're incapable but because we're in love.

I had a legal issue that I had been trying to resolve for several years. I had done time in prison for it, but there was still a civil suit pending that was becoming increasingly more difficult for me to handle. Judy was aware of the case, but I was determined to take care of the issue on my own. Basically, it was *my* problem, and I was going to handle it. Once our relationship went public and Judy began to share more and more about us on social media, I got worried. Judy and I weren't married, but I was concerned that because she was my significant other, the lawyers from the other side of the case would find a way to drag her into the situation because she owns a multimillion-dollar company. And then, what I was dreading happened.

GOLDEN RULE:

"ACCEPT AN OFFER FOR HELP."

There will be times when, no matter how much you think you have things under control, you'll need to set aside your Super(wo)man cape and allow others to help you. Accepting an offer for help from your romantic partner is not an admission that you are incapable of handling things on your own. Rather, it is a testament to your willingness to be vulnerable while recognizing that you do not have to manage everything alone. If you're accustomed to always going it solo, allowing your significant other to help you may feel like a blow to your ego (or relief, depending on the situation). Letting your partner shoulder some of your burden is a sign that you trust them. It also signals to your boo that their support is valued. Accepting help is not a weakness. It's a measure of personal growth where you're open to letting your partner express how much they care for you and want to lighten your load, especially when you need it most.

DaRealBBJudy: I hated that *Beaurtiful* was going through so much drama with the lawsuit. She was determined to fight the case until the day she died, but her decision to stay the course was beginning to have a negative impact on our relationship and our ability to live our lives freely. Plus, we were planning on getting married but had to postpone our plans to keep from giving the other person more leverage against us.

What made matters worse for me is I have always lived an open and unabashed life that includes posting on social media. Since this lawsuit was an ongoing issue, *Beaurtiful* didn't want me to post anything about us. The damn case was lingering over our heads and stifling our lives. The situation intensified when the other party in the case subpoenaed me.

I was tired of our lives being governed by the lawsuit. I told *Beaurtiful* to find out how much we could settle the case for so we could be done with it and move on with our fucking lives. I understood *Beaurtiful*'s intention. She already accepted the punishment for what she had done and spent nearly two years in prison. Her desire to keep fighting was admirable, but I didn't want the situation to hinder our lives any longer. I was determined to convince her to settle the case.

Da Brat: I appreciated that Judy had my back no matter what the circumstances were, but I wanted my team, my lawyers, and me to figure out a resolution or make the lawsuit go away. I also didn't want any of Judy's hard-earned money to be used for a settlement. I thought it wasn't fair, and it was truly fucked up for me to come into the relationship, fall madly in love, and bring my baggage that she would have to carry with me as my future wife. But Judy didn't care about any of that. All she wanted was for that lawsuit to be settled so we could live our lives happily.

DaRealBBJudy: Brat tried very hard to convince me to let her handle it her way. She was persistent in telling me how she didn't want her situation to affect me, but the truth was, it already had. It was also affecting the dynamic between us. I reminded Brat that she had accepted me for all my flaws and told her that our relationship wasn't a one-way street. I wanted a life with her, and that included everything that comes in the package no matter how much it cost.

Da Brat: It was difficult at first for me to accept the fact Judy felt so strongly about settling the case. Her willingness to be a part of the solution taught me a valuable lesson about what it means to lead and follow in a relationship. I thought doing things my way and fighting the good fight was the best way to protect my relationship. But the longer the case continued, the more harm it caused me, my finances, and my love.

To be successful in a relationship, each partner has to be willing to accept that the roles of leading and following are interchangeable. Judy is naturally a problem solver. She pushed me to seek a way out of my problem even though it wasn't what I wanted and cost us money. In the end, the financial cost turned out to be minor compared to the enormous amount of freedom it brought to our lives.

The Takeaway

Every relationship has its own special rhythm. The decision of who will take the lead and who will follow—as well as the specific situations in which each role is appropriate—is unique to your relationship. We have found that what helps us move through life together harmoniously is allowing our individual strengths (and weaknesses) to serve as guideposts for which one of us should assume a specific role and under what circumstances. That may not work for you and your husband/wife/boo/bae/significant other. Creating a peaceful and mutually beneficial atmosphere is the main goal of developing a connection that lasts. As you and your loved one work out the details of who will take the lead and who will follow in various situations or in general, here are a few more golden rules to keep in mind:

1. **Determine the desired outcome.** Knowing from the outset what you want to achieve will help you decide who is the best person to take the lead in a situation. We both wanted to move forward with our lives and get married. We were happily in love, but the ongoing lawsuit was a threat to both of our financial situations. While Brat wanted to keep fighting and believed she could resolve the matter on her own, Judy's decision to help settle the case enabled the desired outcome to become a reality for us.

2. **Push your ego aside.** We are both strong, independent women who can take care of ourselves. Just because we are used to being in control of every situation doesn't mean we have to remain in control, especially if there is someone waiting in the wings who

is willing and able to take the reins. If you're resistant to allowing your partner to step in and take the lead, is your reluctance due to your need to always be in a position of power? Or do you have trust issues, and you're afraid of what could happen?

3. **Create balance.** Be open to compromise by determining and prioritizing what's important to you and the relationship and consult each other before making decisions.

Reflection

Da Brat

Growing up I always had boyfriends. My first crush was a guy named Keith. He came from a big family that was popular in our church. A lot of girls liked him. But Keith made me feel really special because even though all the girls liked him, he liked **me**. Then in high school I was crushing on a guy named Andre. He was a transfer from another school. He was so cute. He liked me, too, but just like Keith, Andre was liked by a whole bunch of girls, too, so I decided I wasn't about to compete for his affection.

Back then I wasn't interested in girls and never knew anything about liking girls. I didn't know what liking girls felt like and didn't even know what lesbianism was. There were older women around me whom I looked up to and wanted to be like, but other than that I wasn't physically attracted to girls. I had no concept of what gay or queer was. I was just a churchgoing little tomboy.

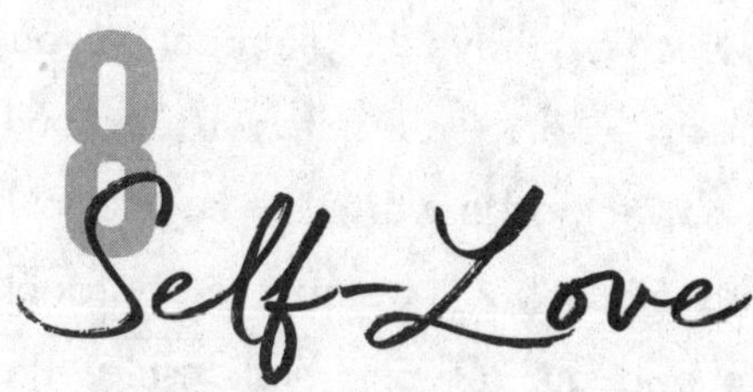

Caring for myself is not self-indulgence, it is self-preservation.

—Audre Lorde

In our roles as wives, girlfriends, partners, mothers, all too often we find ourselves in the position where our needs fall behind the needs of others. There is nothing more true than this for us. In our marriage we've become total experts on loving and supporting each other and now our child. But we are works in progress as we try to make time for our relationship, our careers, our family, and ourselves.

GOLDEN RULE:

"SELF-CRITICISM IS COUNTERPRODUCTIVE."

Negative self-talk is a huge hinderance to personal growth. By undermining your self-confidence, self-criticism can open the door to a fear of failure and make it hard to cope with mistakes. Practicing self-compassion and acceptance will help you create a more positive self-image, which can have a big impact on your romantic relationship. By being kind to yourself, you acknowledge you don't have to be perfect to be worthy of having love in your life. With a healthier mindset you'll be able to approach challenges and setbacks in and out of your relationship with a sense of self-assurance that, regardless of the situation, you are doing the best you can. Embracing self-compassion will also inspire you to extend empathy and understanding toward your significant other because you'll recognize they, too, are doing their best. To nurture a strong and balanced romantic relationship, it's important to always extend some grace to yourself and your partner. Everyone is deserving of it.

DaRealBBJudy: I remember watching the video of Shonda Rhimes giving a commencement speech at Dartmouth College. She said when she's asked how she is able to do it all—be a single mother and a successful TV writer and producer—she said she doesn't. She revealed that whenever she is excelling in one area of her life, she is undoubtedly failing in another. That speech truly resonated with me because it was the absolute truth.

I became a mother for the first time at the age of fifteen and had two more kids before my twentieth birthday. I also miscarried a set of twins. When I was raising my children, I made sure every Sunday that I did something with them, kind of like how my daddy did for me and my siblings. I was brought up in love, and I wanted my children to know love, too. I told them "I love you" all the time and tried to give them everything I could.

With my daughter, I felt a lot of guilt because she didn't have the great dad that I had. I tried as best as I could to make sure she didn't miss out on anything, and there was nothing that she wanted that she didn't get. As I focused on growing my business, it would take a lot of time away from her and her brothers. To make up for it, I would spend as much of my free time with them as I could and do special things. An activity I used to love to do with them was serving breakfast for dinner. I would make a whole buffet. It would be on a random Saturday night, and we would eat nothing but breakfast foods as we watched movies or played games.

Over the years I would struggle with guilt. I could not give my company or my kids 100 percent of my time and attention. In the vein of what Shonda said, if I'm killing it at Kaleidoscope, I'm likely sucking as a mom. Throw in my relationship and now marriage to *Beaurtiful*, and there is even more pressure. I try my hardest to make myself present. I've added things like sending Brat flowers once a month on our anniversary day so she doesn't feel forgotten. I'll make an intentional date night or do something so we can get some time together. Even with the effort, I still hear, "Are you still on your phone?" or "Why do you have to work on Saturdays?"

The pressure of having to be everything to so many people has pushed me to try and find time to love on myself as much as I love on my wife, children, business, and friends. Still, making time for self-love wasn't a balm that fixed all things, especially since I neglected to address some issues from my past that resurfaced and bit me in the ass something awful.

GOLDEN RULE:

"FIND A SAFE AND NONJUDGMENTAL SPACE LIKE COUNSELING OR THERAPY TO EXPLORE YOUR ISSUES."

Seeking a safe and nonjudgmental space like counseling or therapy will be beneficial for your well-being. Therapy and counseling are generally safe spaces that encourage honesty, self-reflection, and an exploration of issues that may be causing you emotional distress. With the guidance of a therapist or counselor, you can address personal issues that may be affecting your professional and personal relationships. Additionally, therapy helps you develop coping mechanisms and practical tools to navigate difficult situations and manage stress. Investing in therapy or counseling can help you take a step toward building a positive self-image and creating a more fulfilling life.

DaRealBBJudy: With so many people and things I am responsible for, I was able to distract myself from a bad experience I had buried in the back of my mind. The memory of this event sent me into a horrible depression. It took going to therapy to help me understand that what I had hidden away was an unhealed childhood trauma, and it was slowly beginning to take me over and put me in a dark place. While I worked on healing this traumatic experience, something my therapist recommended for me to do was to take a photo—not necessarily take a photo of myself, but find a photo—that makes me happy. She told me to come up with four words and add them to the picture then make it my screensaver. The photo I chose was a screenshot of how much my company Kaleidoscope has made to date. My choice might be strange, but I selected my company's earnings because I am proud of what I've accomplished.

Although I thought the exercise was stupid and random at the time, I added the four words that made me feel good about myself and saved the image as the background shot on the home screen of my phone. I chose my phone instead of my computer because the whole world knows I am a phone addict. Staring at my accomplishment multiple times a day did actually help to pull me out of my funk because I was reminded of shit I often forget. It's the stuff I am proud of but don't take the time to ever celebrate.

GOLDEN RULE:

"TAKE PRIDE IN YOUR ACCOMPLISHMENTS."

Celebrating your accomplishments is key to developing self-love and a positive self-image. Taking time to acknowledge your successes, no matter how big or small, can boost your mood and motivate you to continue striving for your goals. Recognizing what you've achieved personally and/or professionally affirms that you have unique talents, strengths, and abilities that are worthy of being celebrated. By acknowledging and celebrating your accomplishments, you are reinforcing the belief in your own potential and capabilities. This positive reinforcement can help you overcome self-doubt and empower you to take risks and pursue new opportunities in life and also love.

DaRealBBJudy: When you're on a journey to love yourself, there's always some amazing things that are buried underneath the things that are so loud. In order to declutter, and to get the loud things out of the way, I needed a regular reminder on the device I look at the most of how amazing I am and all that I have been able to accomplish professionally. The assignment was such a simple little task that I had no idea it would have such an incredible impact on me.

Having a reminder of my own joyous inspiration and determination helped me turn the light back on in my life because I was slowly succumbing to darkness. I appreciated how the task my therapist gave me was like a silent affirmation. I'm not one who will stand in front of a mirror and say a bunch of things, but I will look at my phone.

I think a lot about the many blessings I have and the fearlessness that has been required for me to go after what I wanted professionally with Kaleidoscope and personally by pursuing a relationship with *Beaurtiful.* When I think about where this fearlessness comes from, I am able to pinpoint some things that have happened in my life—from a miscarriage to surviving Hurricane Katrina to getting out of several bad relationships. Getting through those things and others and still being able to say I'm here and I'm fine, I can't help but think, *What is there for me to actually be scared of?* I have a lot of faith in God and believe that anything is possible. I have a certain level of fearlessness *because* of God. But I also think I am fearless because God brought me through some other things.

GOLDEN RULE:

"PRACTICE GRATITUDE."

Gratitude is a positive emotion that directly shapes how you show up in the world for yourself and how you interact with others. Gratitude is a shift in your perspective. Rather than focus on what you don't have, with gratitude your focus turns to all the wonderful things you do have in your life. This little perspective change can do wonders in helping you combat feelings of inadequacy or unworthiness, because it encourages you to show an appreciation for the amazing things in your life, including the people. By embracing a gratitude mindset, you'll begin to see the beauty in all things, recognize silver linings, and appreciate the lessons life teaches you. A shift toward a positive outlook can help you see life through an optimistic and resilient lens, which is sure to have a huge impact on your ability to pursue and maintain healthy relationships with friends, family, and of course your person.

Da Brat: Self-love isn't a concept that I am all too familiar with. My wife always says that she thinks I love her more than I love myself. I don't believe that's true, but I do put her needs and feelings before I put my own because I love her and want her to be happy. I've had some pretty cool relationships. I've dated some famous people. And a couple of those relationships were great, but nothing compares to this. I've never felt *this* loved, and I've never understood love so much before. Maybe I've never paid enough attention?

Or maybe I've never cared enough to pay attention? But I'm very grateful for this relationship because I feel if I had not met Judy and this love had not happened between us, I may not have ever had this experience. Some people never find this in their whole lifetime. I must have done something good somewhere because God has certainly blessed me with an amazing life and wife.

GOLDEN RULE:

"MAKE CHOICES THAT FEEL RIGHT TO YOU."

Prioritizing your own needs and desires is an act of self-love and self-care. By making choices that align with your authentic self, you affirm that you not only know what you want but also trust yourself to make decisions with confidence and without hesitation. One of the greatest gifts of being in tune with yourself is that it becomes easier to prioritize your needs rather than sacrificing them to accommodate others. Trusting yourself, honoring what you want or need, and making choices that reflect your values and desires ensures that self-care is not just an idea or an afterthought but a fundamental necessity in your life regardless of whether you are in a romantic relationship or not.

Da Brat: I can truly say that I am the happiest I've ever been in my life. I was forty-eight years old and pregnant. I had two doctors before Judy and I became pregnant tell us there would be no way for me to carry a child. But we beat the odds. Now I have a beautiful, healthy baby boy. Judy always says my desire to focus on her and our family reminds her of Vanessa Bell Calloway's character in the movie *Coming to America*. Judy says that like Princess Imani Izzi, whenever she asks me anything, my response is "Whatever you want." I dislike it when she draws that comparison because I'm not brainless like the character. I know my wife means no harm, but I am making a conscious choice to dote on my family. Judy often asks me what I want to do, places I want to go, and I honestly don't care as long as I'm with her and things are happy and good. I've already done so many things during the span of my career. I don't have the desire to go jump out of a plane or take a trip inside an active volcano. If that's what she wants to do or plan for us, then I'll say yes. But my happiness isn't doing things. It's being with her.

GOLDEN RULE:

"LET YOUR CREATIVE ENERGY FLOW."

Creativity and honoring one's unique talents are important aspects of self-love. By allowing yourself to explore your creative side, you give yourself permission to express what lights your inner fire. Whether it's through art, music, writing, or any other form of expression, tapping into your creative energy is a therapeutic activity that connects you with yourself on a deeper level. Expressing creativity can also provide a personal outlet for you and your partner to nurture yourselves outside of the relationship. Creative activities are a gift of self-discovery via self-expression that you can share with your partner to offer them insight into another side of you.

Da Brat: Other than our life together, the one thing that makes me happy is music. But I don't get to do that much at all between work and caring for True. I still enjoy being creative and writing songs for other people, whether they're R&B or rap songs. I have a studio in our house, but my schedule is often so busy that I don't have a lot of time to create musically.

When I was younger, all I wanted was to be a good musician and performer. But God can bring new things into your life that mean just as much to you as the things you used to really enjoy. Right now for me it's my wife and son.

I love being a mommy. I don't have time to sit in the studio as much as I did before, but when I do go in there, I write and record lullabies for our son. I'm working on a few projects for him because I love him so much. If anything, that's my self-love. It's a release for me. But I also enjoy my jobs. I love doing the radio show every morning. I love shooting *Dish Nation* and talking about a variety of topics. And when I come home, I want to spend time with two of the most important people in my life—True and Judy.

The Takeaway

Theoretically, a self-love and self-care routine should be in place before entering into a committed relationship. In real life, things aren't that cut and dried. What usually happens is that being in a committed relationship teaches you the importance of self-care. There's something about the intensity of emotional and romantic intimacy, having to be mindful of someone else's wants and needs while also being supportive of their ambitions, that exposes our own weak spots.

When you're trying to go the distance in a romantic relationship, having areas where you may feel inadequate or, worse, unfulfilled, can have a negative impact on your relationship. For example, not feeling good about how you look can make sexual intimacy less enjoyable with your partner or influence you to avoid intimacy altogether. Spending too much time catering to another person's needs while neglecting your own can lead to resentment and conflicts.

While we love being together, we've definitely learned that self-love and self-care looks different to each of us. We may not have spa dates or even get that much alone time these days with a little one now in the picture, but we do try to tap into what brings us joy. Just knowing that much has made a huge difference in our being able to keep our relationship, and by default each other, free from having to deal with intense feelings of anger, frustration, envy, jealousy, and resentment. Here are a few more golden rules to make sure you are taking care of yourself in your relationship:

1. **Have your own damn thing.** A relationship is a part of your life, but it should not be your entire life. Don't lose sight of the things or people that were important to you prior to becoming boo'd up. Pursuing your hobbies, passions, and goals will help nourish your spirit so your relationship can thrive. Maintaining a healthy balance between your personal life and your relationship is the best way to achieve long-term happiness and fulfillment.

2. **Embrace optimism.** Shit will hit the fan from time to time, but keeping an optimistic outlook will do wonders for your overall health and well-being. Plus, a positive mindset will make your interactions with your partner more enjoyable and productive. A funky attitude is definitely a turnoff and can put an unnecessary strain on your relationship. You are entitled to feel all the feels, but positivity makes self-care a daily ritual by reducing stress and lifting your spirits. The better you feel, the better you are able to be present in your relationship.

3. **Get some sleep.** Rest is a primary form of self-care. Your body and mind need to recharge daily in order to function properly. The lack of sleep on a regular basis will make you more irritable, stressed, and burned out. There's no way you will be able to maintain a healthy relationship if you are not healthy. So take your ass to bed at night.

4. **Reclaim your time.** Taking care of yourself isn't selfish, but it could make your loved ones feel like you're neglecting them when you choose your own needs over theirs. Although it may

be challenging at first, learning to say no becomes easier the more you establish healthy boundaries. If you want to keep your romantic and personal relationships strong and avoid feelings of exhaustion and resentment, be honest about your needs and limitations. Just because you say no doesn't imply you don't care; it just means you need to spend time caring for yourself and your needs.

9 Prioritizing Each Other

It took us two tries at this thing called love before we were able to get it right. Our first attempt at coupledom came to a screeching halt for reasons we don't need to rehash. Besides, you already know who's to blame. Even with the disappointing first try, our relationship did have some beautiful moments where we both were eager to show how much we liked each other. With several failed relationships under each of our belts, our decision to spin the block and give this relationship thing a second go-round is when we became decidedly relentless in our commitment to demonstrate how much we really wanted this relationship to work and how important we were to each other.

GOLDEN RULE:

"MAKE A BIG IMPRESSION."

Making a big impression is a fantastic way for you and your significant other to nurture your relationship. Whether you plan a surprise getaway or simply write them a heartfelt note, these thoughtful gestures will show your partner how much you care, appreciate them, and want to make them happy. Every act of love and consideration is an expression of your commitment to the relationship, but making a big impression every now and then adds a layer of excitement and unpredictability that will keep things from becoming too mundane. Taking the time to plan something special for your partner shows that you value them and are willing to put in the time and effort to create lasting memories. These meaningful moments serve as a reminder of why you chose each other and want to continue building a life together.

DaRealBBJudy: After letting Brat know that I was interested in her, I was eager to impress her and show her that I meant business. I wanted to give her flowers for Valentine's Day, so I reached out to her personal assistant to find out the best place to send them. She has so many jobs and nobody wants to give you any information in case you're a stalker or something. But I got the address and asked my assistant to purchase the flowers for me and make sure they were sent on the day.

Valentine's Day rolls around, and I'm excited. I just knew my flowers were going to make a big splash. I'm steadily checking social media to see if she's gonna post about receiving them. Apparently, *Beaurtiful* is extremely popular because she posted like six or seven different floral arrangements she received from her "admirers." But there wasn't anything posted that acknowledged receiving a gift from me. We weren't public with our courtship, but she had done work for Kaleidoscope so receiving flowers from me wouldn't have made anyone think something was going on between us.

So I'm looking at all the floral arrangements she received, and I'm trying to figure out which set of flowers she'd posted was from me. I checked in with my assistant and asked her what kind of flowers she sent her. She told me she sent her some flowers in a box kind of shit that she had ordered online from 1-800-Flowers. Everyone knows I'm extra. If I'm going to do something, I am always going to go big. I was expecting my assistant to have sent her the kind of bougie flowers I normally send that are in some special kind of setup. But no ma'am. That's not what she did. My assistant sent her some regular ole flowers in a box that didn't even come with a vase and water. Like, WTF?

At some point *Beaurtiful* did mention on her social media that she received my box flowers, but I felt really stupid. My flowers didn't make a lasting impression like I'd hoped on the day you're supposed to show the person you like or are in love with how much they mean to you. But I was determined to make my mark. I ordered her eight boxes of the Forever Flowers and sent them to her job. Now these flowers were totally bougie! I had them customized so they spelled out her name. Each box had a letter for her name spelled out in roses. It was a beautiful setup. I was not about to have her thinking I sent her some fucked-up flowers.

GOLDEN RULE:

"BE GRATEFUL FOR SECOND CHANCES."

Being grateful for a second chance acknowledges the value of forgiveness and growth in a relationship. It shows that both parties are willing to move forward, rebuild trust, and strengthen the love connection. Second chances require maturity and humility from both partners, as it takes courage to move past transgressions, make amends, and actively learn from past mistakes. But an expression of gratitude shouldn't be the only way to show appreciation for another opportunity to make your love thang a success. Making a consistent effort through your words and actions will demonstrate your renewed commitment to nurture each other and the relationship. Additionally, second chances shouldn't solely be about not repeating past mistakes. It's about putting forth the effort to make sure mutual admiration, support, and love become the foundation of your togetherness. By prioritizing these values, you'll be better positioned to build a more loving and sustainable partnership.

Da Brat: The flowers Judy sent to my job at *Dish Nation* were the talk of the office. I was working with Porsha Williams at the time, and she said, "Biiiiiitch, who got you those!? These are some expensive flowers, like $500 a box." I told her they were from a girl I was kinda talking to. Porsha was so over-the-top about those flowers and in her excitement for me. Everyone who saw them said they were beautiful. I had never heard of Forever Flowers, so I didn't know how big of a deal they were. It really was a beautiful gift and gesture. I was happy that Judy left that stankin'-ass ex of hers, and it opened the door for us to rekindle our friendship. I was hopeful that we would finally become a couple. After receiving her bougie flowers, I was confident in the future.

GOLDEN RULE:

"PRIORITIZE BEING FRIENDS."

Friendship is a strong foundation for any romantic relationship, as it helps establish a deep connection based on genuine likability and compatibility rather than physical attraction. While attraction may initially spark the friendship, developing a platonic bond first allows your relationship to progress naturally, giving you ample time to get to know each other without the added pressure and expectation of physical intimacy. A romantic relationship rooted in friendship is more likely to succeed, as the framework for healthy communication, support, and mutual respect has had the opportunity to develop first. Once romance takes root, the strong base built through friendship can serve as the launching pad for a fulfilling partnership where love and intimacy can grow in tandem with the bond you've already built.

DaRealBBJudy: I didn't leave my situation with the stankin'-ass man, as *Beaurtiful* puts it, to be with her. I left the relationship because it was so toxic, and I needed to leave for me. I left my own house and even the furniture in it to get out of that horrible situation. I just moved out and walked away. The situation between him and me got so bad that I had to compensate him $100,000 to basically remove him from my life. Because of that, I went on social media and announced that my company was having what I called a "Bitch-Ass Nigga" sale. I was angry and venting, so I made up a discount code. It was "BAN." The good news was that after having to write a check to get this person out of my life, I made $137,000 back from the sale.

The best part of that breakup was that it brought *Beaurtiful* back into my life. She saw all the stuff that was happening on social media and reached out to check on me. From that point forward we were reconnected. However, we didn't just jump back into dating. We prioritized being friends. It was easy for us to fall into a relationship because the attraction was still there. Unlike before, the second time around we were both actively putting in the energy to make our relationship succeed.

GOLDEN RULE:

"DON'T BE AFRAID TO RISK EMBARRASSMENT."

Risking embarrassment for love might sound daunting and totally unappealing, but some of the most powerful moments in a relationship stem from an act of boldness or pure honesty. Stepping outside of your comfort zone with a grand romantic gesture, a heartfelt confession, or a burst of playful silliness can create defining experiences that leave lasting imprints of bravery and vulnerability. These shared instances of authenticity signal a commitment to allowing yourselves to be seen in all your glory—quirks and all. Embarrassment isn't always enjoyable, but an honest display of emotion or realness is an invitation for you and your beloved to forge ahead with a connection built on trust, acceptance, and unconditional love. The most meaningful relationships aren't built on perfection, but on the courage that it's okay to be imperfect and adored anyway.

Da Brat: I was ready and willing to do anything for Judy. After we had committed to taking the relationship to the next level, Judy decided to uproot herself from New Orleans to come be with me in Atlanta and had gotten herself a condo. I still had my own place, but I would often spend my nights with her. There was this one time that her toilet got clogged, and she couldn't fix it. I wasn't there at the time it happened, but Judy had eaten something that tore her belly up! She went to the bathroom and shit up a storm. She shit so much that it clogged the toilet. She had been plunging for dear life before I got there but still wasn't able to release the clog. When I walked in the door Judy told me not to use the bathroom. When I asked her why, she explained what had happened. She was so embarrassed. I couldn't stop laughing. We had gotten serious and even a shit-filled toilet wasn't gonna stop me from showing her that she was my person and there wasn't anything I wouldn't do for her, including unclogging a shit-filled toilet.

DaRealBBJudy: One of the most beautiful moments I ever experienced with *Beaurtiful* happened a couple of years ago when I had gotten sick. This illness came out of nowhere. We weren't married at the time, but she dropped everything to tend to me. I spent time in the hospital. At one point we didn't know what the prognosis was gonna end up being or which way things were gonna turn. But *Beaurtiful* completely went into caretaker mode. She was making plans and suggested that we hurry up and get married in case something happened. It affirmed for me how blessed I am to have her standing by my side. She never thinks twice when it comes to being there and caring for me. I am blessed to have that, and I don't take it for granted.

The Takeaway

Not every couple gets a second chance to figure out how to make a relationship succeed. We consider ourselves lucky that it was in the cards for us to have a future together. The decision to move forward with a relationship despite the disappointing first start enabled us to focus on being friends, learn to communicate, spend quality time, and prioritize appreciating each other. A healthy relationship requires mutual effort. Here are a few more golden rules to help you make your partner's happiness and relationship nonnegotiable:

1. **Be direct. Tell your partner what you want.** Prioritizing a partner and a relationship might seem like a no-brainer, but every person has unique needs and wants. Instead of letting your partner "figure it out," speak up and tell them what makes you feel valued in a relationship. A road map of what makes you feel loved, appreciated, heard, and seen is the perfect jumping-off point to build a healthy relationship.

2. **Take action.** After you and your partner have communicated your values and expectations for each other, the next step is to put this knowledge into action. Set boundaries for yourself so you can be consistent with prioritizing your time as well as their needs. You may need to do regular check-ins to make sure you both feel the relationship is progressing in a healthy manner or to readjust your boundaries.

3. **Lead with love.** Things will go wrong, and important dates or times may be forgotten. Don't always think the worst of your person or the situation. Please allow each other the space to be human and make things right. Assuming your partner dropped the ball on purpose or doesn't care about your needs is not helpful if you want to build a good relationship that lasts. Revisit the conversation about what you need to feel loved and supported. If the issues continue, we're recommending that you lead with love not stupidity.

Reflection

DaRealBBJudy

When my dad got ill, I noticed that my mother didn't change. She continued doing all the things she had been doing for my dad, and it didn't matter that he had become frail and was no longer able to be the breadwinner. When my dad was placed on dialysis and my parents had to sleep in separate bedrooms because the dialysis machine was so loud, my mom never stopped caring for him. She would make sure my dad got into the bed and was hooked up to the machine before she would lay her head down to sleep. She did all the things that she was supposed to do for someone you love.

Until my father's death, I watched my parents enjoy each other, love each other, and express love to each other. If it's true that a child will mimic what they experienced during their childhood, then I have been looking for that kind of love my entire life.

10 Growing Together

At some point, most people (and it doesn't matter if they are gay or not) have heard the joke about lesbians. *What does a lesbian bring to a second date? A U-Haul!* Okay . . . so, it's not a total knee-slapper, but it does touch on a phenomenon in the LGBTQIA+ community where lesbians are known for jumping into serious relationships quickly. Basically, lesbian relationships work like this: "I like you, you like me . . . now we're wifeys." Seems crazy? Well, it happens—a lot actually. We'll have you know that we bucked that trend. Living in different cities helped us with that.

While the U-Haul joke is common in LGBTQIA+ humor, we feel it's a regular occurrence in most modern relationships no matter what side of the sexuality fence you sit on. It's understandable because shit has been discovered in the dating pool. Sound the alarms! If you're as lucky as we have been to find a romantic partner who is likable, available, and sane (hopefully), the urge to lock the relationship down is pretty hard to resist—gay, straight, or otherwise.

GOLDEN RULE:

"ALLOW THE RELATIONSHIP TO CHART ITS OWN COURSE."

A relationship has its own compass, so you don't have to steer it all the time. Trust in the connection you share and allow it to guide you to whatever destination you are meant to reach. Let go of the need to control every aspect of the journey and instead focus on building a strong foundation of trust, communication, and respect. It's not about who's steering the ship but about the journey you take together. Trust in each other and let the relationship navigate its own course. Allow each other the space to move comfortably through the relationship and for the next steps to develop naturally without constant pressure for either partner to take the helm. A relationship is a shared experience. Embrace the process of growth and discovery so you and your partner can navigate the journey together, ensuring your relationship evolves in alignment with your shared vision and values.

Whether you've been together for two weeks, two months, or two years, conversations about next steps for how you will grow in your relationship are never a bad idea. Despite living in different cities for several months into our relationship, we were able to avoid the inevitable pressure couples doing the long-distance thing feel to accelerate the growth of the relationship. We let our romantic bond deepen at a steady pace. It undoubtedly helped that the distance between Atlanta and New Orleans isn't that great, but we can say for sure that our ability to get along easily and the strong feelings we have for each other played a significant role in us being able to strengthen our connection and get to forever without having to sacrifice our respective careers and passions for the love.

DaRealBBJudy: The funniest thing about our relationship is that we never actually formalized becoming a couple. After my breakup and we got back in touch, we didn't rush to date. We were friends first, then the relationship just happened. We never officially asked each other to be in a relationship. We didn't say, "Would you be my girlfriend?" We just knew being together felt right. Even as we were living in separate cities, there was never a conversation about me moving to Atlanta.

My business was steadily growing just as the relationship with *Beaurtiful* was taking off. I was happy living in New Orleans, but professionally I was feeling like I needed to be somewhere else and outside my norm. I wanted to be around people who would inspire me to reach for higher. New Orleans is a wonderful place, but I knew for my business to continue to grow that I would have to change my setting. I narrowed my choices down to three cities—Miami, Atlanta, and Houston.

I would slide into each of the cities to get a feel for them. I'd already lived in Houston for a short time after Hurricane Katrina. I was familiar with the city although I didn't live there very long. Atlanta quickly moved to the top of my list as our relationship started to progress, but I didn't make the decision immediately. It was over a span of months that I mulled over which city to relocate to. Even with *Beaurtiful* being in Atlanta, moving there wasn't a foregone conclusion. I wanted to be closer to her, but I also wanted to do what was right for me and my business.

In addition to my love interest living there, Atlanta had a lot of perks that were attractive to me. First, it's the mecca for Black entrepreneurs. The homes are also unlike anything I've ever seen in my life. New Orleans doesn't have the kinds of homes you see in Atlanta. Everywhere you go, it's like four-story palaces. These ain't no regular-ass houses here. I wasn't just trying to find the right city for me to grow my business, I wanted to be in a city that motivated me and pushed me to take my life and my business to the next level.

Obviously, being in the same city would have been ideal for our relationship, but *Beaurtiful* didn't press me to choose Atlanta. She's not pushy like that. Before anything else, she's a supportive friend. She'd ask, "What do you think? What do you feel is best?" Even if I hadn't chosen Atlanta, we would probably still have continued to date. But Atlanta won out because it's a city where Black people are thriving. I am inspired here. When I drive around I am encouraged to do more and to keep striving. The other side of my decision was that my love was here, and I wanted our relationship to succeed just as much as my business.

GOLDEN RULE:

"MAKE SURE YOU'RE ON THE SAME PAGE."

The decisions to date exclusively, cohabitate, get married, or have children are major milestones in a relationship. Before you and your significant other decide to take a big leap that will further embed you into each other's life, it's important to have a serious heart-to-heart to ensure you're on the same page about what may lie ahead. Sharing your thoughts with each other and clarifying how you'll handle potential situations as a couple will prevent you from bumping heads unnecessarily. You'll be better able to navigate the inevitable ups and downs in your relationship when you and your partner are clear on how you expect to move forward. Being on the same page doesn't mean you have to agree on everything, but it ensures that, as a couple, you have a clear intention of how you will work together to achieve mutual goals while also supporting each other's individual endeavors.

DaRealBBJudy: A lot of the major things that have happened in our relationship have been the result of us just being spontaneous in how we interact. We love each other so much that we actually fall into situations but not on purpose. Getting pregnant was one of those instances. One night *Beaurtiful* asked me to go out with her. I don't remember where. But we are almost always inseparable. I was in a playful mood, and in response to her question I said not only would I go anywhere with her, I would even have her baby! That was the first time I ever brought up having kids with *Beaurtiful*. I've been a mom for a long time. My kids are adults. They are all about to be moved out of the house. One even has their own child. I thought I was finished raising babies. I never said to myself or anyone that I would never do it again, but I certainly wasn't *looking* to do it. But being in love is a powerful feeling. Ain't nothing more serious than having a child with someone.

In that moment I wanted *Beaurtiful* to know that I was happily down for forever and whatever with her. I was being lighthearted, but that simple comment was the beginning of us having more in-depth conversations to explore what having a child together would mean for us and our future.

Da Brat: It was about two years from the time in the condo when Judy said she would have my baby before it came up again. The more we mulled the idea over, one thing would always remain a constant. If we were to have a baby together, then Judy would be the one to get pregnant because she has had the experience already. I'll be honest, having a baby was not something I ever planned on doing. When my career kicked off I was still a teenager and I was super busy being a rap star. Back then I was out there having sex and even missed my period a few times, but I was fortunate that there were never any pregnancies. Also, I was such a granny's girl that had I gotten pregnant when I was younger, she would *not* have been happy with me because that's not how I was raised. Growing up in her sanctified home, the expectation was that I would follow God's rules. First you get saved, marriage follows, and then and only then do you have a baby.

With my music career being my primary focus for most of my adult life, the idea of me having a baby just didn't feel like a possibility. As time moved on and I'd gotten older, it seemed that a child wasn't in the cards for me. And, at my big age, physically it was even less likely. Since Judy is a few years younger than I am, it made all the sense in the world that if we proceeded with having a child together, she would be the one to carry it. I just didn't expect that the internet would have such a huge impact on us deciding to actually move forward with our child plans but also on me believing motherhood *was* for me.

DaRealBBJudy: Someone on the Kaleidoscope marketing team came up with a great idea for a campaign to help promote the launch of a product. The plan was for the announcement to appear like Brat and I were expanding our family but the new addition was actually my product. To make the campaign as realistic as possible, we took photos like we were in a doctor's office having an ultrasound. Instead of an image of a fetus in the womb, we set it up so that the image on the ultrasound screen would be a photo of the product.

Beaurtiful and I took a selfie together for the campaign to make it look real. She wrapped her arms around my waist, and we placed our fingers together to form a heart on my belly. To kick off the campaign, in January 2022 I posted the selfie and added the caption "We are extending our family." Of course, the photo went viral. We were featured on Yahoo! News and many other websites and blogs. Thousands of people, including other celebrities, offered their congratulations on our "announcement." The photo created a huge splash, but it wasn't what everyone thought it was about.

GOLDEN RULE:

"BE OPEN TO NEW POSSIBILITIES."

Allow yourself to be stretched. Embrace the challenge of doing something you never imagined. When you try new things or take risks, you'll grow as a person while uncovering new passions or abilities you never expected. This step toward personal growth won't just benefit you, but will also positively impact your relationship. When you and your significant other approach life with curiosity and an open mind, it will keep your relationship from becoming stagnant. Growth is an important aspect of life. Resisting self-discovery can lead to complacency, which will unfortunately have a negative impact on your relationship. By keeping the door open to new experiences, you invite adventure, excitement, and a renewed sense of passion into your life and relationship, ensuring that both have the much-needed opportunity to evolve and thrive.

DaRealBBJudy: Since everyone was already thinking that we were going to have a child, *Beaurtiful* asked me if we should seriously consider doing it. I had already told her that I would have her baby. She just needed to get on board with the idea. I believe the response from the public really helped her get comfortable with the idea of becoming a mother. So many of the comments we received on the photo were supportive of her taking the journey into motherhood. A lot of people—not just those who knew her personally—posted how great of a mommy she was going to be because she's naturally very nurturing. With so much support coming our way, *Beaurtiful* was persuaded to do it for real.

From the moment we fell in love, I was willing to have a

child and do anything with her and for her, but there was one condition—I told her that if we were going to do it, we needed to do it sooner than later. Once we decided to move forward with having a child and actually expand our family for real, I never released the marketing campaign. It was a great idea, but it didn't make much sense to put stuff out there about this new product when we had decided to take the biggest step in our relationship since getting married.

GOLDEN RULE:

"DON'T GET DISCOURAGED."

As your relationship progresses, the inevitable difficulties that come your way may feel impossible to navigate. There will be moments of disappointment, miscommunication, and other challenges that you'll face as a couple and individually that will test your patience and commitment to staying the course. It's easy to surrender to feeling discouraged when things fail to go smoothly. However, a positive outlook can help to keep you from wallowing in despair. Instead of seeing the obstacles in your life or relationship as signs of gloom or doom, view them as catalysts for growth. Disagreements can lead to better communication, mistakes bring wisdom, and problems build resilience. No life or relationship will be free of hardships. How you and your partner choose to handle the difficulties is what matters most. Focus on creating a supportive atmosphere no matter what's going on. Relationships thrive not because they are always easy, but because both partners remain committed to supporting each other's personal development, maintaining a closeness, and moving forward despite the hard times.

DaRealBBJudy: Once the decision was official that we were moving forward with having a baby together, we had to get educated on what the next steps would be. We went to see different doctors. One doctor we were referred to was very insensitive to us as an LGBTQIA+ couple. We were sitting close to each other holding hands. It was obvious that we were together. Even some of the people who worked in his office were fans of *Beaurtiful*'s and knew we were in a relationship. But the doctor wouldn't acknowledge us and repeatedly asked about a "boyfriend."

Da Brat: We were told he was supposed to be this really great doctor, but his insensitivity toward us as an LGBTQIA+ couple wanting to have a baby made us both feel so uncomfortable. First, he told me that because I was in my forties, I was too old to have a child. I already knew my age could be an issue, but this doctor's bedside manner left a lot to be desired. The way he disregarded us as a couple was totally inconsiderate.

If one thing's for sure and two things are for certain, I know God's an on-time God. I learned that much growing up with my granny. Judy and I were invited to an event at the Old Lady Gang, the restaurant owned by Kandi Burruss, a singer-songwriter from Xscape and my longtime friend.

Left: The day we met, at Judy's tour stop in Atlanta.
—Brat

Right: The day we shared our first kiss, on the side of Morrow's restaurant.
—Brat

Above: The day I gave my crew (*left to right*: Phil Thornton, friend and music exec; Bella Wilkinson, management; Jermel "Flick" Evans, security, with glasses, standing behind us; and Mister Overstreet, lil' bro who performs with me) a heart attack by holding hands out loud at the Essence Festival with Judy. —Brat

Judy watching me perform (So So Def, me, and Jermaine Dupri) from the side of the stage at the Essence Festival. —Brat

(Photos on this page courtesy of the authors)

Our first photo
shoot together.
—Brat

She always gives me major butterflies.
—Brat

(Photography by Will Sterling)

Our Christmas photo shoot. *(Photography by Will Sterling)*

Bottom left: The PARADE in New Orleans when I sat right in front of her on a FLOAT. So PROUD.

—Brat

Bottom right: The first birthday of mine that we celebrated while living together in our new home.

—Brat

(Photos above courtesy of the authors)

Representing my commitment to our everlasting love. Here is the tattoo on my back of our wedding date, 2.22.22. —Brat

Judy posing in her wedding dress. (*Inset*: Our wedding date monogram on the venue floor.)

(Photography by Stanley Babb with Stanlo Photography)

One of the exquisite tables at our wedding reception venue.

Our beautiful photos of us together at our wedding.

(Photography by Stanley Babb with Stanlo Photography)

Both of us reentering the venue, after Brat's outfit change.

(Photography by Stanley Babb with Stanlo Photography)

A close-up of us during our maternity photo shoot.

Pregnant Brat and Judy.

Judy holding my stomach during our maternity photo shoot.

Brat celebrating her forty-ninth birthday with a photo from her maternity shoot.

(Photography by Derek Blanks with crowdMGMT)

Our family newborn photos. (*Left to right:* Brat, True, and Judy.)

Bottom left: Our all-gold photo shoot.

Bottom right: Our 2024 photo shoot.

(Photography by Derek Blanks with crowdMGMT)

Dr. Jackie Walters was at the event as well. In addition to being a star on the show *Married to Medicine*, Dr. Jackie is an OB-GYN. Dr. Jackie came up to us and said whenever you're ready to have a baby, I'm your doctor. After that shitty experience with the insensitive doctor, running into Dr. Jackie was definitely a part of God's plan. Dr. Jackie referred us to Dr. Obehi Asemota at Hope Fertility, who became our IVF specialist. Working with Dr. Obehi was such a blessing. She and her team were so nurturing. They talked us through everything and made us feel comfortable. It was like we were meant to be there.

DaRealBBJudy: Full workups were done on the both of us to check the health of our bodies and our egg quality so we would know all the options that were available. The tests showed that either one of us could carry. I still had healthy eggs, but unfortunately *Beaurtiful* didn't have many eggs left. But I felt in my heart that since I had already had the experience of being pregnant, I should talk to *Beaurtiful* about adjusting our plans to allow her the opportunity to get pregnant and have our child.

• • •

Growing together isn't just deciding when, if, or how you and your partner will move forward in life together. The big "couple" moments are important and a fundamental part of growing together, but another way to strengthen your foundation and sustain your love connection is to make sure there's room in the relationship for you both to become the best versions of yourselves. The goal for every healthy relationship, at least as we see it, is not to stifle each other. How in the hell are you supposed to grow as a unit if one or even the both of you are stagnant?

It's definitely a cliché, but growth is an integral component of life. Sometimes, in this thing called love, you may see an opportunity for your partner that they never even imagined for themselves.

DaRealBBJudy: We were taking our dogs for a walk while filming our show. I had been thinking about telling *Beaurtiful* that even though the doctor said I had more healthy eggs, I really believed that she should be the one to carry our child instead of me. The moment I said this to her it was like everything came to a sudden stop and a needle was being scratched over a record. All *Beaurtiful* could say was "Wwwwhaaaatt!" I knew suggesting that she carry would come as a surprise after telling her several times that I would have a baby for her, but my reason for wanting to change up the plan was solid.

Initially, *Beaurtiful* wasn't trying to hear any of what I had to say. Despite her immediate resistance, I pressed on. I broke it down like this—I know her. Like, I really know her. What I also knew was how big of a deal having a baby was going to be for our life, and I was confident in my belief that she would really love the experience. My suggestion that she be the one to carry our child wasn't because I didn't want to do it. I just knew that *she* would love it. The love that you feel and the bond that you develop with your baby when they are inside of you is indescribable. I knew in my heart it would be an amazing journey for her. She just needed to work through the fear.

Da Brat: When Judy said she thought I should carry our child, all I could think of was *Why me?* I'm like the dude in the relationship, and now she thinks I should carry a baby? I then started to wonder if she was suggesting that I be the one to get pregnant because she didn't want to go through the process again after already having several pregnancies. But I knew in my heart that that wasn't how she actually felt. But I was so unsure about doing it. Not to get all graphic or anything, but I had this big fear that my "pocketbook" or "hoo ha" was gonna split open. Shit, every time you see a woman having a baby, they're crying and screaming for dear life and they want to kill somebody because it hurts so bad.

Just thinking about what happens in childbirth had me scared as shit, and I really did not want to go through it. We continued to talk through my fears. Our conversations really helped me get comfortable with the idea until I finally said, "Okay, I'm gonna do it." When our IVF doctor confirmed that my uterus was crisp and clean for me to carry Judy's egg (or be the oven, as I like to say), I was thrilled. I don't have anything against surrogacy, but I really wanted us both to feel attached to our child.

Looking back on our childbirth journey, I have to say how grateful I am for Judy's love and support. She opened the door for me to experience something I never in my life believed would or could happen. Judy recognized that I had fears but never wavered in her belief that I would have an amazing, life-changing experience. And she was right.

Being pregnant with our son, True, was the best experience in the world. There really is nothing and no love like becoming a mother. I appreciate my wife for encouraging me to face my fears and be open to the journey, which taught me so much about myself. My biggest lesson was that I am a lot stronger than I thought. Pregnancy is no joke. I got carpal tunnel in both hands. My ankles were swollen most of the time. My toes were folding like Vienna sausages. Toward the end of the pregnancy my coochie bone was throbbing constantly. But I didn't complain about anything because it was more important to me to cherish every moment—the good and the bad. But I truly enjoyed the process just as Judy said that I would.

The Takeaway

Growing together isn't just about being able to take momentous steps in life together. It's also about creating the opportunity for you and your partner to learn more about yourselves both as individuals and collectively as a couple. The journey to building a relationship that lasts will require a commitment to creating and sustaining a supportive environment that enables you both to reach your full potential as you strengthen your love for each other. Here are some other golden rules to keep in mind:

1. **Check in with each other.** Be up-front and talk about the things you want for yourself and the relationship. If you are on the same page, it'll be easier for you to support each other as you move toward your goals as individuals and as partners. However, if you find that you have different ideas or plans for the future, you'll need to have a conversation about how you can work through those differences while nurturing the relationship and each other.

2. **Let resilience become your superpower.** There will always be obstacles. Commit to seeing things through to the end no matter the outcome.

3. **Always be willing to collaborate.** You're a movement by yourself, but you're a force when you're together. 'Nuff said.

Reflection

Da Brat

Though I grew up in a superreligious household, the idea of me growing up, finding a husband, getting married, and having kids was never forced on me. My grandmother would sometimes talk about me having my own family when I was older, but it was never an idea that she or anyone required of me.

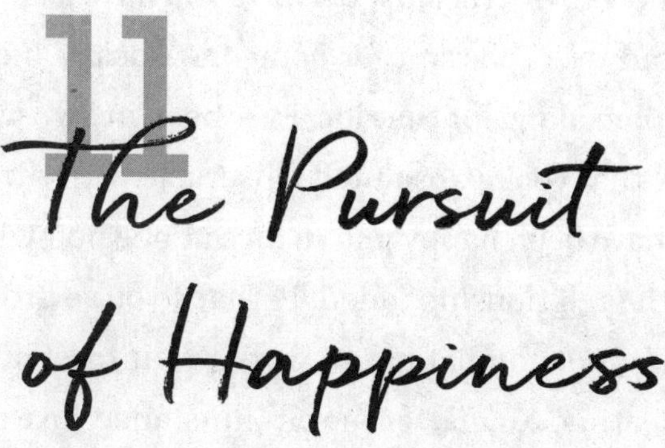

11 The Pursuit of Happiness

A lesson we have learned not just from choosing each other but in building a life together is that in relationships (and life in general), love and happiness are not the same. Like the pastors do in church, we're gonna say it one mo' gin for the members of the congregation sitting in the back who came in late—**LOVE AND HAPPINESS ARE NOT THE SAME.** Amen? *Amen!* No matter what type of 'ship you're in right now—romantic relationship, partnership, friendship, situationship—whatever word you choose to call it, the sooner this little life lesson registers in your brain, the better off you'll be to achieve the important goal of finding, nurturing, or building a relationship that lasts and is affirming.

So why is it important to understand that love and happiness are not bonded at the hip? We're no psychologists. We're just two lesbians who have been fortunate to experience some things, and the simplest answer we can offer is that in relationships, there's no guarantee for either.

Here's what we know to be true: Just because you have feelings of love, attraction, and even passion for someone doesn't mean that happiness will come along for the ride. Ever been in love with a person but discover that you're absolutely miserable with them? To be fair, you could have been happy and in love at one point, but over time the joy in the relationship faded. Perhaps you've grown apart, discovered you're not compatible, or worse, your trust bond was broken due to cheating. No matter the circumstance, love can exist in a relationship without happiness. The opposite is also true. Just because you experience incredible feelings of happiness when you're with someone does not mean you are in love. What's sad is that a lot of people confuse the two. The joy of companionship, mutual respect, and feelings of contentment don't always translate to romantic love. There's a lot of folks unable to get out of the friend zone for this very reason. Ever had someone in your life who clearly wants something romantic with you, but you don't like them in the same way? Somebody cue up a soulful rendition of the song "I Can't Make You Love Me."

Another aspect to this topic that we can't leave out is that, as the saying goes, "happiness is an inside job." In other words, happiness comes from within. That means no one person is responsible for whether you feel happy. Putting the onus on someone else is the guaranteed path to frustration, anger, and disillusionment because the bus to your personal happy place is driven solely by you.

However, in relationships, each person bears a responsibility for contributing to the environment so that happiness can thrive.

As we've shared throughout this book, we are both grateful to have found an amazing partner in life and love. This is the best relationship either of us has ever been in. Because we've both survived prior relationships that weren't fulfilling, the key factor for us being able to foster love ***and*** happiness in each other has been understanding the role authenticity, responsibility, and accountability play in making ours a happy home.

GOLDEN RULE:

"DEFINE YOUR NEEDS."

Clarifying your needs is an important step in building a strong, lasting relationship. When you and your significant other understand and respect each other's priorities, you can work together to meet those needs and build a partnership based on mutual care and appreciation. If you haven't had a conversation about your expectations, what makes you happy, deal-breakers, and your personal and shared goals, make it a priority. Knowing what each of you values and needs allows you to be more intentional in how you engage with and support each other. Having a dialogue about these key elements for you in a relationship should not be a one-and-done discussion, but an ongoing conversation. As you both change and grow, your needs may evolve as well. Regular check-ins with each other will ensure that neither of you is operating in the dark. Compromise should also play a role in how you and your partner move forward, but it shouldn't mean consistently sacrificing your own well-being. To strike the right balance, you may need to adjust expectations occasionally, but without abandoning your core values. By investing time to understand each other's emotional, physical, and intellectual needs, you'll create a foundation for your relationship that's sturdy enough to support the both of you.

DaRealBBJudy: The saying goes that you kiss a lot of frogs before you find your prince(ss), and that is definitely true in my case. I was previously in another long-term relationship that was riddled with issues. I had reached my breaking point and wanted out but didn't take any action to remove myself and my children from the situation. I kept telling myself that if I continued to shower my former partner with love that the relationship would improve. It didn't. The only thing that grew were my feelings of misery.

While there were many issues in the relationship, there was a theme that would surface regularly that would trigger intense emotions. I'm a very generous person. I often think about others, sometimes even before myself. That's just the way I am wired. A huge pet peeve is when people are selfish and inconsiderate. I'm the type of person who, if I'm ordering food and there are seven people in my house, I'm ordering for everyone. It doesn't matter the cost. It's the considerate thing to do. But I was in a relationship with someone who didn't see courteousness in the same way that I did. I remember several occasions when they would be heading home after work and would stop off at a restaurant to pick up food. You would think it is a no-brainer to get food for everyone in the household, but they wouldn't. They would buy food solely for themselves. To some, that might not be a big thing, but it is a huge red flag to me and was a guarantee that I would be in my feelings. You went to a damn restaurant and got food for yourself and didn't think to text or call the person you're in a relationship with to see if they are hungry? Even if I am not hungry and don't want or need any food, I'd still like my partner to ask. It's a common courtesy.

GOLDEN RULE:

"NURTURE TO BE NURTURED."

A relationship where both partners nurture each other produces a supportive environment for personal growth and development. When partners encourage and empower each other to pursue their goals, explore their passions, and overcome challenges, it creates a safe space for both to thrive and reach their full potential. Nurturing each other also strengthens the foundation of the relationship. Consistently showing care, kindness, and affection toward each other builds a solid framework of love and support that can withstand life's ups and downs by providing stability and security. Beyond emotional support, nurturing each other also means being an active listener, offering comfort during difficult times, and finding ways to inspire your partner. Nurturing can take many forms. Words of encouragement, thoughtful gestures, and physical affection can make your partner feel loved and supported during the good and bad times. Consistent acts of love, no matter how large or small, deepen intimacy and will draw you closer together. By prioritizing each other's needs and actively working to support and uplift each other, you and your partner can create an environment where you both can experience and enjoy a profound sense of connection and fulfillment.

DaRealBBJudy: It's always been important to me to find a relationship where I am not only loved but seen and heard. Like in my parents' marriage, I've wanted a partner who not only feels that I am a priority in their life but acts like it. That is one of the qualities about my relationship and marriage to *Beaurtiful* that touches my heart and fills me with happiness. As her wife and life partner, not only am I a priority to *Beaurtiful*, but my feelings matter to her. I have no doubt at all that my wife would step in front of a bullet for me or fall on a sword if it meant it would protect me. There is hardly a time when she doesn't make me feel special, thought about, seen, and heard. That was not the case in my other relationships.

When we first got our house in Atlanta, *Beaurtiful* still had her own place and she would go back and forth between the two residences. One year for Thanksgiving, I went home to New Orleans—but I wasn't feeling it. I wanted to be back in Atlanta to be closer to her, so I did a quick turnaround trip and came on back to Atlanta. *Beaurtiful* was with her family and friends, so I returned to our newly purchased fifteen-thousand-square-foot home. It was quiet in the house, and I got spooked every time I heard a sound. I was on the phone with *Beaurtiful*, and I told her I was hungry. She didn't understand why I wouldn't just go down to the kitchen to get myself something to eat. The reality was I was in the bedroom with the door closed, petrified. It was frightening to be in that big ole house by myself.

Beaurtiful kept me company on the phone for a good long while until she said she had to call me back. A short time later, she showed up at the door with Thanksgiving food for me in hand. She left her people to come be with me because I was scared. That moment was so special and still means so much to me. I didn't have to ask her to leave her gathering to come be with me. I wasn't even expecting that she would do it. But the fact that she did it because she wanted to spoke to her love and desire to meet my needs whether they're articulated or not.

GOLDEN RULE:

"SHOW APPRECIATION FOR ALL THINGS LARGE AND SMALL."

Expressing gratitude reinforces positive behavior and strengthens the emotional connection between partners. By acknowledging each other's efforts, no matter how big or small, it encourages more of the same. This cycle of appreciation helps establish a supportive and loving environment where you both put forth a regular effort to make each other feel valued and appreciated. Keep in mind that gratitude is more than just saying "thank you." Gratitude can be demonstrated through your actions as well. Thoughtful gestures, kind words, and acts of service should be woven into your daily interactions, as they are key expressions of affection and care. For your romantic relationship to thrive, showing, communicating, and feeling appreciation should be a focal point in how you and your partner interact with each other on a consistent basis.

Da Brat: I spent most of my younger years with both of my grandmothers. My maternal grandmother would give a person the shirt off her back. If she only had ten dollars, she would give away nine and keep one dollar for herself. She did the same with food. Whatever she had, she would give most of it away and keep a tiny bit for her to eat, and she would be content with that.

My paternal grandmother was just as loving. When I was failing in school, she talked my mother into letting me come live with her, so I could go to a school closer to her home.

I enjoyed being my grandmothers' baby. They both had such big hearts that I vowed that I would give them the world. When my rap career took off, that's exactly what I did. Whatever they wanted, it was my pleasure to give it to them. Pedicures, money, trips . . . whatever made them happy I would do because they took care of everyone. To me, grandmothers are the most amazing beings in the world. It hurt me deeply when both of mine passed away. I often would find myself missing their loving, giving spirits in my life. And then I met Judy.

Judy is the ultimate giver. My love language is acts of service but hers is gift giving. As she says all the time, giving makes her heart smile. To an outsider, being on the receiving end of this type of love expression may look easy, but it wasn't for me.

The first big surprise gift Judy gave me was back in 2020. It was shortly after the photo was posted that marked my coming out. I remember some weird stuff was happening with our garage. I was told there was a problem with the remote and the door wasn't opening. I went outside and Judy came and stood next to me. The garage door opened and inside was a Bentley Bentayga SUV with a big red bow on it.

Now, I have been wanting this car forever. When I realized what was happening, I started backing up. I wanted to run. Judy used all her body weight to prevent me from escaping. She kept saying, "Nope, you don't get to run." But I did. I took off. First, I don't know how to accept gifts. I also don't like people doing such major things like that for me. I needed Judy to know that I didn't care about the things she could buy or do. I just wanted her.

Looking at that car and knowing that she bought it for me tore me apart. My next move was to run inside the house. Judy ran after me. I went back outside, got in my Jeep, and locked the door so I could cry my eyes out. And there I was, boo-hooing. No one had ever given me a gift like that. No one had ever gone through the trouble of planning a surprise for me like that.

Plus, I had so many questions. How did she and everyone around us keep that shit a secret? (I have since learned that Judy doesn't play any games when it comes to planning surprises. Everyone is sworn to secrecy.) I was so emotional trying to figure out how it all happened. When did she put the car in the garage? How did I not notice anything going on?

I made a video of me ugly crying in my car. Even though I was looking crazy, I posted the video. I had all these feelings I was trying to articulate. I remember thinking this woman is incredible. How did I get to be so lucky to be in love with someone so thoughtful and generous? I remember saying to Judy, "You bought me a fucking car? Not just a regular car but a Bentley, my dream car?"

I accepted this gift, but there had been many other gifts

from her that I had rejected. Not long after we met and were getting to know each other, I was working on some music at the So So Def recording studio. Judy was sitting there with me, and she had her wardrobe stylist come bring me this huge bag with clothes, shoes, and a bunch of accessories from Fendi. I refused to accept it. I made her take it all back. Actually, to make her happy, I kept the shades. I still have them, too. But the bag the wardrobe stylist brought in for me was worth thousands of dollars, and there was no way I was going to accept it.

DaRealBBJudy: The story is that Fendi had just dropped this collection that I wanted. My wardrobe stylist went and grabbed some pieces for me. I told my stylist to grab things they thought would fit *Beaurtiful* and her personality. I was already buying stuff for myself so why not shop for her, too? He did what I asked and he bought all these amazing items like a Fendi trench coat and pieces to go with it. There was a hat, tennis shoes, glasses, a scarf, and gloves. My stylist brought them into the studio, but *Beaurtiful*'s reaction was not what I'd hoped it would be. First of all, we weren't alone, and there were quite a few people in the studio with us. In front of everyone, she said, "Take it all back!" I was embarrassed and wondered what I'd done wrong.

Beaurtiful's answer at the time is one I still hear from her regularly, which is that she doesn't need anything. We had been getting to know each other, and during that time she had witnessed people using me. These were people that I thought were friends, but they had other motives. I understood that *Beaurtiful* wanted me to see that she wasn't like those people and that she was only interested in me as a person and not the things I could buy. But knowing that she doesn't want anything from me makes me want to give her everything.

GOLDEN RULE:

"UNDERSTAND WHOM YOU'RE IN A RELATIONSHIP WITH."

Understanding whom you're in a relationship with and what makes them tick is a worthwhile investment in the health, stability, and longevity of your relationship. Love languages provide valuable insight into how your partner likes to show and receive love. Recognizing and adapting to these preferences will go a long way in maintaining harmony and strengthening your romantic connection. However, not every display of love and affection may feel natural or comfortable to you. What matters is being able to find the balance between honoring your boundaries and understanding how your partner engages with you. Besides love languages, truly knowing your partner means understanding other things, too, such as how they handle conflict and stress. Being attentive to their habits, communication style, and emotional triggers will help you respond with empathy instead of frustration, which can incite unnecessary drama. The way you respond to your partner in all situations significantly impacts how secure and valued they feel. By acknowledging that you both have past experiences that shape your perspectives, you'll set the tone for respect, patience, and kindness to prevail. It will take being intentional about factoring in everything from each other's love languages and life history to make sure your relationship is grounded in love, support, and mutual understanding.

Da Brat: It's still hard for me to receive the gifts Judy gives me, but I've gotten way better at accepting them. I really had to change my mindset about it all. Giving gifts to me and others makes her happy. I didn't know anything about love languages when I met her. Since then, I've learned that a person's love language is how they give and receive love. Being able to shower me with gifts makes her happy. I thought turning her gifts down was showing her that she means more to me than the gifts she gives and that I'm not like other people who have taken advantage of her and her big heart. But if there's anyone who should understand how much it means to her to gift me things from her heart, it should be me. It's not easy and I'm always shocked by her surprises. Judy lives by the slogan "Go big or go home." And she goes big on everything! You would think that by now I would be able to catch on when she's planning something major, but she gets me every fucking time.

GOLDEN RULE:

"DON'T LET SMALL ISSUES BECOME BIG ISSUES."

At first, some issues or annoyances may seem insignificant, but if left unaddressed, they can fester and escalate into something that can eventually tear the relationship apart. Avoiding confrontation over what seems like a "small" issue is setting yourself and the relationship up for failure. If something bothers you, it's better to address it early rather than let frustration build and lead to an unnecessary conflict. A small issue can't be resolved if it goes unmentioned, so make it mandatory that you both check in and discuss any and all concerns as they happen. Being able to talk to each other openly without judgment will make sure what needs to be addressed is discussed and resolved. It's also important during these conversations to acknowledge each other's feelings. One of you may think something is minor, but if your partner brought it to your attention, then it obviously matters to them. Listen intently, respond calmly, and try to find a compromise to maintain the health of your relationship. Relationships require that each person be willing to put forth the effort to keep small problems from turning a good partnership into a problematic shit show. Dealing with small problems as they come up shows that you both are committed to having a regular open and honest dialogue to keep the air between you free of resentment and animosity.

Cultivating happiness in our relationship hasn't only been about keeping things positive and joyful all the time. Disagreements in our household are few and far between, and that's largely because we try to resolve any grievances we may have with each other fairly quickly to avoid small issues from becoming big issues and big issues from becoming even bigger issues.

DaRealBBJudy: A few years ago when my youngest son moved in to live with us, things got really challenging. I was a teenager when

I started having children, so how I raised them is different from the kind of mother I am now. As a young, working single mom, I had housekeepers who would come and clean the house two or three times a week because I didn't have time to wash the clothes and do all the other things parents do. And, since I was doing everything I could to keep a roof over my head for my children, I didn't hold them accountable to do too many chores while they were growing up. *Beaurtiful*, who was raised differently than how my kids and I were raised, felt it didn't matter what my son didn't have to do as a child, but as an adult living in the home with us, he needed to take on more responsibility.

Da Brat: We were filming our show, and one time I found myself expressing my feelings about how I think her son should do more around the house. Judy was sitting next to me, but I wasn't looking at her. As I'm rambling on she had actually gotten upset and started crying. She got up and walked out of the room. I was like, "Oh my God!" I was just going on and on about how I felt and wasn't even thinking about the impact my words were having on her.

When she walked out on me in the middle of the conversation, I felt like shit. I immediately followed behind her to go talk to her. She explained to me why my words hurt her. There's no perfect way to be a parent, and everything I was saying about how her son lacked basic skills when it came to helping around the house, Judy received as a judgment of her parenting skills. After listening to what she had to say, I felt even shittier.

What Judy shared made a lot of sense. Since I wasn't a parent at that time, it never dawned on me how it would feel to a mother to have someone speak about what her adult child hadn't learned when he was young.

It is never my intent to hurt my wife's feelings in any way. And though I didn't think what I was saying was hurtful or judgmental, that doesn't mean it wasn't interpreted that way. No relationship is perfect. And I'm certainly not. I do dumb things sometimes. I was so disappointed in myself during that incident. It was important that I apologize and take accountability for how my words hurt Judy despite my intent.

GOLDEN RULE:

"MAKE YOUR TIME TOGETHER A GOOD TIME."

Making every moment you and your partner spend together a good time is an absolute must. Not only does it contribute to a positive and joyful environment, but it reinforces that you are in sync and genuinely enjoy making each other happy. When you know that time you spend together is fulfilling, no matter what you choose to do, it alleviates pressure and allows you and your significant other to simply relax and appreciate being in each other's company. Whether you're trying out a new hobby together, going on spontaneous adventures, or simply having a movie night at home, finding joy in each other's company is fundamental to a successful and fulfilling relationship. The moments of fun and laughter you create should bring you closer and set the tone for how your quality time should feel. In addition to planned activities like weekly date nights, your day-to-day interactions are equally important to the health of your relationship. The goal should be that even the most routine tasks are enjoyable because you're together. Affection, laughter, and good conversation are great benchmarks for quality couple time that nourishes both your spirits.

What often comes as a surprise to many people is that though we are a celebrity couple and our life is chronicled on our own TV show, we're not the type of famous personalities who are in the streets a lot. We are basically homebodies. Now that we're raising a beautiful little boy, there are even fewer opportunities for us to partake in the glitz and glamor of the celebrity lifestyle. It doesn't matter if we're home watching movies or on a fancy vacation, happiness is always when we're spending time together.

The Takeaway

If you're lucky enough to have found love, you have a choice to make about whether you'll be happy, too. Love and happiness don't always go together, but there are things you can do to usher in happiness and keep love alive at the same time. Keep in mind that love is often tied to intimacy, but few people remain open to intimacy if they don't consistently feel heard, considered, and respected. Here are a few more golden rules to help your pursuit of happiness take shape:

1. **Be authentic.** If you aren't authentic, you can't be truly known and understood. If you feel unknown by your partner, you won't feel loved from the outside in. If your partner's love doesn't

reach you, unhappiness can set in. Here's the thing: If you don't know yourself, how can you be authentic? Getting to the core of who you are might mean you have to peel back some layers and endure some discomfort as you learn to love yourself from the inside out. That's when you become more authentic. Knowing yourself makes it more likely that someone else can get to know you well, too.

2. **Share your truth.** Conversations about your backstory can enrich the relationship and foster a sense of closeness so long as you leave space for your partner to reciprocate. Nothing can replace the depth of knowledge you'll gain about your partner from spending years together and paying attention to how they think and act every day. However, you can deepen your understanding of each other more quickly by openly sharing your journey of self-discovery through past relationships, family experiences, and other pivotal life moments. Being willing to share these aspects of yourself with the person you want to know you best requires trust, honesty, and vulnerability. There may be some things you want to keep private, but if you want a relationship where you're seen and loved, sharing intimate details can be a guiding light for your partner.

3. **Discover love languages.** There's a reason millions of people have taken the Love Language Quiz. It's an easy way to learn how you best like to interact in love. After answering a series of questions, you'll receive an assessment of your preferred expressions. The Love Languages model is based on the idea that

there are five categories: physical touch, quality time, receiving gifts, acts of service, and words of affirmation. Your results are ranked from strongest to weakest to help identify what resonates most with you. You may learn that you prefer to be told "I love you" more than spending alone time together, or that acts of service carry more weight than physical touch. Understanding each other's languages is like having a relationship manual with instructions on how to make your partner feel loved and valued. Without these key insights, maintaining happiness in your relationship can become a challenge.

4. **Utilize what you know.** Learning about your partner's authentic self and love languages gives you both the opportunity and the responsibility to be more considerate and intentional in the relationship. Now that you know whom you're sleeping next to, whom you're making travel plans with, who's next to you in the car, and who's sitting across from you at the kitchen table, you can no longer claim ignorance. How you treat each other is a direct reflection of what you've learned. Excuses won't build a happy partnership, but healthy communication, honesty, and a concerted effort will. Consistently making choices that align with how you both expect and deserve to be treated reinforces that happiness in a relationship isn't elusive. It's both attainable and sustainable.

12 Never Stop Dating

Thus far we've shared many of our golden rules for maintaining a healthy relationship. But here's a truth bomb: This shit ain't always easy. It is a rare occurrence, that is, if it happens at all, for either one of us to wake up in the morning, choose violence, and pick a fight. Thankfully, that's not how we get down. But we are aware that no matter how deeply in love we are and plan to stay, to ensure that we succeed at this thing everyone in the entire world is hoping to find, we have got to (in the words of Rihanna) "work . . . work . . . work . . . work . . . work."

GOLDEN RULE:

"BE HONEST ABOUT THE CHALLENGES."

Being honest about the challenges in a relationship is crucial to its long-term success. When you and your significant other are comfortable sharing your thoughts and feelings about your struggles or the lackluster areas in your relationship, it can lead to a stronger connection as you both can address concerns and make changes if needed. Open discussions about the challenges or difficulties give you the opportunity to demonstrate teamwork and create the type of partnership that aligns with your needs and expectations. Instead of letting difficulties push you apart or allowing frustrations to build, honest communication puts you both in a position to take responsibility for the relationship and work to preserve it. Acknowledging that there are issues that are adversely affecting your partnership doesn't mean the relationship is on a path to failure. However, it does enable you both to show how much you care about each other and your commitment, so the relationship survives despite the difficulties. There will inevitably be struggles that will test your ability to get along, but having an open line of communication can make those times far less stressful and more manageable. If you and your partner are willing to be honest, work together, and address each other's needs, challenges in the relationship can become opportunities for a stronger bond rather than sources of division.

We agreed long before we walked down the aisle that we would prioritize keeping our love connection intact by doting on each other and spending quality time together. While we always have the best intentions, there have been some occasions where we have fallen short because between the two of us there's a shit ton of responsibilities on our plates. There's managing and growing a successful hair-products business, coproducing and shooting a reality TV show, and cohosting a daily TV show and syndicated radio program. As if that weren't enough, we went and added the biggest responsibility of all—having a child. We're exhausted just thinking about it all. Because our daily schedules are often booked from sunup to sundown, finding the time for each other to go out on date nights or spend uninterrupted time together has been an ongoing struggle.

DaRealBBJudy: I work from home but *Beaurtiful* does not. She gets up superearly in the morning to go do *The Rickey Smiley Morning Show*, and after that she's off to record *Dish Nation*. When she comes home in the early afternoon, she's done with work, but I am not. My workday is still going. Sometimes my head gets cloudy because I have so many things to do. I actually have to sit still and do nothing for ten minutes just so I can gather my thoughts on the best way for me to attack my long to-do list. When *Beaurtiful*'s workday is over she gets to come home and relax. At times I think she forgets that I'm still in the middle of my day so I can't switch my focus to our couple time as quickly as she would like.

Da Brat: It has been a source of frustration for me that my baby is so busy and I feel like I don't get enough of her attention. I've since learned how to deal with it and hold my peace and wait until she has time for me, but getting to a place where I am able to wait my turn has been a process. I remember several years ago we had traveled to either New York or Los Angeles. Here we are in another town for an event, and I couldn't get any time with her because she was preoccupied with Kaleidoscope stuff. Now, they don't call me Da Brat for nothing. I'm spoiled. I can admit it. And I had a fucking meltdown. We were lying in the bed, and I told her "I'm not getting enough attention from you." I was totally in my feelings, whiny and saying things like I didn't feel like she loved me enough. I didn't really believe that, but I was feeling completely neglected because I wasn't getting quality time with her because she was working. Then, when she wasn't focusing on work and was sitting still, she had her phone in her hand.

I remember how saddened Judy was after I complained about feeling neglected. She ran down for me what she was doing and then said she was trying to get everything done so she could give me the attention I needed. It was important for me to express my feelings, but once I did I felt some kind of way about it. I could see that she had a lot going on and was struggling to get everything handled. She obviously was feeling some pressure and my complaint only added to it because there was yet another demand on her time and energy.

DaRealBBJudy: In the beginning, it was very hard for *Beaurtiful* to understand that being on my phone doesn't mean that I am mindlessly scrolling. I use my phone a lot for my business. Though it looks like I'm scrolling, the reality is I'm probably doing something related to my business like writing a caption, watching a video that needs to be edited, or responding to the dozens of emails I receive every day.

I understand how frustrating it can be to get time with me. When I wake up in the mornings, I turn over and get right to the emails. I might not move and sit in the same spot from the time that I wake up until the time she gets home. There are many times when I'll have my assistant bring me food because I don't move around that much.

When we first got together I could tell that *Beaurtiful* had difficulty understanding how I worked and what my work was. It was a huge challenge for me because as much as I wanted to change how things were for me and my business, I couldn't (and still can't). I've created this monster of a responsibility for myself, and I couldn't just change it. But I had fallen in love with someone whose situation was 1,000 percent opposite from mine. I had to go to God about it. I prayed and said, "God, if this is for me, I need you to work out some kind of terms. We got to figure this out! You placed this big vision on my heart and in my life. The train is rolling, and now this person is here. If this person is from you, then they're gonna have to connect in some kind of way."

Though I wanted to put my phone down more, what I ended up doing instead was updating *Beaurtiful* with details of everything my team and I had going on. Now she gets it. She understands why I'm up at two o'clock in the morning doing inventory management or a check run or balancing out the numbers for the year. My goal for three years has been to have less on my plate so I can be more present with *Beaurtiful.* In that same time my company has grown, so instead of there being less on my plate, there's more.

Da Brat: After my meltdown I had a talk with myself. I decided I didn't want to be the kind of spouse who puts pressure on their partner and makes their life more stressful. I wasn't deciding to put my needs on the back burner, but I did realize that being a pain in the ass wasn't going to help me, her, or our relationship. I promised myself that going forward, I would switch gears and be the support she needs by offering her my patience, love, and consideration. It didn't happen overnight. It has taken me a minute to get to a place where I am able to tame my spoiled brat tendencies and exercise some patience and understanding.

The thing that helped me was acknowledging that I can't do any of the shit that she does. I tried to put myself in her shoes, and I couldn't fill them. I don't know how she manages to do all the things and still find time for me, our son, and her older kids. She has to attend Zoom meetings with ten different people to discuss the products, hire new employees, fire ones who aren't doing their jobs, market the business, develop new products, and a whole lot more. I already knew that she was an amazing woman, but I had a newfound appreciation for how truly incredible she is, and I'm extremely proud of her. I am cool about waiting my turn. When she does get to step away, I am grateful that I get to kiss her, hug her, and do whatever she needs that makes her smile. The best part is she does the same for me.

GOLDEN RULE:

"FIGURE OUT WHAT WORKS."

Figuring out what works for a relationship is a process of trial and error. There is no one-size-fits-all answer, as what works for one couple may not work for another. It's important for you and your significant other to communicate openly and honestly with each other about your needs and expectations in the relationship. This process may involve setting boundaries, compromising, and being open to feedback. A willingness to try new things and make adjustments along the way can help you strike the right balance. It's also crucial for both partners to show empathy and understanding toward each other's feelings and perspectives. By continuously working on the relationship and being committed to growth and improvement, you and your significant other can ensure your relationship is always a place of peace and enjoyment instead of ongoing strife. Nurturing your relationship with love, patience, and understanding will lead to a strong and lasting connection that is something special that you allow to evolve alongside your busy lives.

Watching other celebrity couples, including those who aren't famous, doom spiral and share the grievances they have with their partners on the internet serves as a reminder for us to find ways that are unique to us to keep the love flowing. Our situation started out differently than your average couple. First, as we mentioned earlier, we lived in different cities so we had to navigate getting to know each other from long distance. Then there was also the issue of keeping our relationship private since Brat was still in the closet. Given the things we have had to endure, dating looks somewhat different to us than other couples.

What works well in our relationship is creating memorable moments and doing things for each other that include spending time together. Our intent is to make sure we never forget what we like about each other, why we fell in love, and why we are perfect for each other.

GOLDEN RULE:

"MAKE THEM FEEL SPECIAL."

Making each other feel special is extremely important in a romantic relationship. It shows that you care about your significant other and genuinely want to see them happy. Thoughtful gestures, kind words of support, and physical touch are a few ways to make your partner feel special. Your actions, whether they're big or small, can show your partner that you are paying attention and that you value uplifting their spirits by making them feel loved, appreciated, and supported. Small gestures like leaving a sweet note to let them know you are thinking of them or planning a surprise date night can make a huge difference in how your partner feels. Grand gestures are also wonderful, but consistent thoughtfulness affirms that while their experiences change from day to day, your love, appreciation, and support remain unwavering. Validation and acknowledgment can go a long way in making a person feel truly loved. Making your partner feel special isn't about putting a smile on their face in the moment, it's about creating a lasting, fulfilling relationship where love and appreciation are heartfelt, expressed regularly, and always reciprocated.

DaRealBBJudy: The time I gifted *Beaurtiful* with the Bentley Bentayga was a special moment for her, but it was my way of showing her that no matter how busy I may be, I am always paying attention.

I knew to buy her that car because she had a little toy model version of it. It was white on the outside and red on the inside. I asked her once why she had the toy car, and she said it was the car she liked and wanted to get. Every time she mentions something that I believe is meaningful or important, I tuck it away in the back of my mind. I don't immediately get to work and prepare to make things happen that she mentions on a day-to-day basis. I just listen and wait for the right moment to do something with the info I've retained. I also don't tell anybody when I'm about to take action. I normally don't want input from anyone unless I actually need information they may have to make the special moment happen.

A few years ago I reached out to *Beaurtiful*'s aunt who handles all of her financial and business affairs. I was interested in buying the house that *Beaurtiful* grew up in. She spoke all the time about growing up with her granny in that home, and I thought it would mean a lot to her if she owned it. Since her aunt still lives in Chicago, I knew I was going to need her help to pull this surprise off because a house is not like a car that I can have delivered to our door. Having boots on the ground in the city was going to make things easier.

When I reached out to her aunt and asked her about buying the house, she thought it was a thoughtful idea, but after thinking about it more, she determined it would become too much of a headache to maintain. I didn't make the purchase, but that's not to say that I might not reconsider buying it for her in the future. If I do, she'll never know it's happening.

Da Brat: My baby definitely takes the prize when it comes to giving gifts and creating special moments, but I've been able to surprise her a few times as well. Everyone who watches our TV show, *Brat Loves Judy*, saw the elaborate *Coming to America*–themed surprise birthday party/marriage proposal she put together. She made sure all of our close friends and family were in attendance for what became the biggest moment in both our lives. But I feel like every woman should be able to say that someone got down on one knee and proposed to them, so I planned a surprise fortieth birthday party and proposal for her, too.

I'm not as crafty in the planning process as my wife, but I did steal her phone and get all her numbers. I called a bunch of her really good friends and told them about my plans. The night of the party I told Judy we were going out to eat, but I blindfolded her so she couldn't see where we were going. When we got to the event location, I took the blindfold off, and she was surprised to see all of her close friends in the room, including her son Byron, who lives in Texas.

I wanted the party to be a big celebration, so I had acrobats hanging from the ceiling and strippers in cages. The theme of the party was "40 Shades of Judy." The room was set up with a runway like at New York Fashion Week. As part of the celebration, everyone was told to dress like Judy, and we had a huge fashion show of everyone showcasing their Judy-inspired outfits. After pushing through my nerves I got down on my knees and asked Judy to marry me. I put a diamond ring on her finger so we both would have rings in addition to the experience of a heartfelt proposal.

GOLDEN RULE:

"CATCH THEM BY SURPRISE."

Surprises not only show your partner that you are thinking of them and that you care, but they're also a great way to add excitement and spontaneity to a relationship. There are lots of ways to surprise your significant other, but the best surprises are often the ones that are tailored to their individual interests and preferences. Surprises don't have to be extravagant. Small, unexpected gestures can have the same impact as grand ones. The key to a successful surprise is to pay attention to the little things your partner enjoys and incorporate them into the unexpected moment. However, the most important aspect of the surprise is not what you do but the thoughtfulness behind it. Your significant other will appreciate that you took the time to plan something special for them, even if it is not something they would have chosen for themselves. The element of surprise adds an extra layer of excitement, which will keep things between you fresh and spontaneous. The effort you put into surprising your partner will not go unnoticed. The smile that lights up their face and the gratitude in their eyes will make all your efforts worthwhile every time.

If there's anything that has become a cornerstone of our relationship, it would be surprises. We enjoy making each other feel loved, special, needed, and understood. Surprises enable us to add a little spontaneity and excitement into our lives. There's also nothing like catching the other off guard with something special that they had no idea was coming.

Da Brat: We had so much going on during the planning of our wedding that we decided we would wait to go on a honeymoon. We weren't only exhausted physically by trying to put everything together, we were also exhausted financially. The wedding ended up costing over half a million dollars. We had not planned for that to be the budget at all. Our intent was to get through the wedding then just chill afterward. But my baby loves to surprise me in front of everybody. She likes seeing my reaction and making me cry. I think she enjoys seeing my vulnerable side.

We had made the decision to put a pause on the honeymoon, but at the end of our wedding reception she decides she'll catch me off guard and throw in a surprise in front of everybody. The minute Judy said, "I have something to tell you . . ." my response was, "Oh God!" We were on a stage in front of all these people, and Keith Sweat had just finished singing. I'm like, *What is going on? What is she about to do?* In front of everyone Judy says she has a surprise for me—a honeymoon trip to Turks and Caicos. She got me once again. She planned a trip for us to get away, and, of course, I knew nothing about any of it.

DaRealBBJudy: Though I am guilty as charged of doing the most and surprising *Beaurtiful* with many over-the-top gifts, for me it's the everyday type of thoughtfulness that becomes the most special. One year for Mother's Day *Beaurtiful* set up a tent in our backyard. She put balloons and a bed inside so we could lounge and pillow-talk like we often do. The tent was done so nicely and was so thoughtful. I kept trying to figure out how *Beaurtiful* was able to get the tent set up in the backyard and put a bed inside of it while I was in the house. I'm still not sure how she pulled it off without me seeing any of it.

What I appreciate about how *Beaurtiful* shows her love is that while my gifts and surprises are meaningful but often on the extravagant side, she really has figured out how to touch a special place in my heart with her loving gestures.

Every morning she gets up and leaves for work before I wake up. One morning I had our son in the bed with me. He wasn't feeling well, and he would only sleep if I was holding him. Due to the way I was positioned on the bed, I wasn't able to reach the baby station without waking our son. I dozed off and woke to find that *Beaurtiful* had set up a whole new station for me that was within reach. She put wipes, diapers, a warm bottle, and even the television remote control close to me so I wouldn't have to move or wake the baby.

After long days running Kaleidoscope, to relax I like to sit in the bathtub for long stretches of time. Two hours will pass and you can find me still in there soaking. Since my workload has doubled, I have stopped taking long baths. I said something in passing about wishing I could take my laptop in the tub with me so I could multitask. So I could get back to my favorite relaxation activity, *Beaurtiful* surprised me with one of those sturdy bathtub trays that can hold a laptop. Now I can go back to sitting in the tub for a long time while using my computer. It's always the little things that mean the most because it shows how much she thinks about me, supports me, and loves me.

Da Brat: Judy says I'm thoughtful in my daily actions, but she is the same. She has been so supportive of my journey as a first time mommy. Many times when I'm taking care of the baby she'll go into the kitchen and cook a variety of things. Breakfast foods are definitely a favorite go-to. She'll cook three different types of eggs, bacon, sausage, and pancakes and bring a plate to me and tell me she'll take over caring for the baby so I can go eat. I also love how she calls me *Beaurtiful* every day. And even when she's going through something with the company and she's frustrated or unhappy, the minute I walk into the room she lights up. It makes me feel so good inside and I love that my presence affects her in a positive way, especially if she's going through something.

GOLDEN RULE:

"TURN THE INTIMACY UP."

Intimacy isn't just about sex or physical closeness but also emotional connection and communication. Take the time to listen to your partner, express your feelings, and engage in activities that bring you closer together. Whether it's spending a quiet night indoors having deep conversations about meaningful topics, planning a fun vacation to a tropical island, or sharing daily moments of affection like holding hands or sending each other text messages to check in, any form of intimate gesture will help you maintain a healthy relationship. Creating intimate moments requires an intentional effort. It's also important to be mindful of timing and context. While you might think "whenever, wherever, whatever" is a good approach, make sure your partner is game. Otherwise, what was intended to be an intimate moment can become awkward or, worse, a source of embarrassment. Vulnerability is another way to ramp up the intimacy. Let your partner in! Keep in mind that intimacy is also a two-way street. Reciprocating your partner's gestures will make sure that those special moments together are fulfilling for the both of you.

It doesn't matter how long you've been with your significant other; every relationship goes through peaks and valleys. It sucks, but the newness and joy of finding someone who rocks your boat (pun intended, keep reading) always fades. It's a part of the romance journey, and it happens to everyone. But it's like once you and your boo are locked in, the initial hot and heavy eventually becomes tepid and routine.

The sole reason for making time to date each other regardless of your status (married, committed, dating) is to maintain the love connection at all costs. Ain't no better way to do that than to actually connect—body parts, that is. Making time for sexual intimacy is a must, but adding a little spice here and there to your regular routine will help keep the relationship fun and flavorful.

DaRealBBJudy: Normally, *Beaurtiful* is really shy. She's always respectful and reserved when it comes to affection and sexual things. It's likely due to the superreligious upbringing she had. But while on our honeymoon in Turks and Caicos she showed me another side. It's safe to say a time was had! We spent an entire day on a yacht, and despite there being other people on the boat with us, *Beaurtiful* and I were in our own world.

Da Brat: There was a bedroom near the bathroom just below the top deck of the yacht. I had this really cute furry cover for us and lots of pretty pillows. I slid her panties off and that was my dinner! The boat was already rocking, so we rocked the boat some more.

DaRealBBJudy: There was another time when we were on the top deck of a boat that wasn't covered. Everybody who passed by our boat got a show! *Beaurtiful*'s typically not a risk-taker like that. But it's nice every now and then when I get to see and experience another side of her. It's exciting, and it makes being together intimately even more enjoyable.

The Takeaway

Relationships are like plants. If you want yours to grow, you must feed it. If you want it to grow healthily, you're gonna have to nurture it. Just because all appears to be well between you and your significant other does not mean you get to check out and let the relationship operate on autopilot. Energy is needed to keep things moving. Finding time to date each other (or dote on each other, as we like to call it) is a terrific way to keep your hearts aflutter, strengthen your commitment, and create a pathway to lasting love. Here are a few more golden rules to help you keep the good vibes flowing in your relationship despite the many things you've got going on:

1. **Decide your "special" time.** As far as we can tell, no one has figured out how to add a few more hours to the clock, so even with

a ton of things on your plate every day, you're going to have to "Just do it," as Nike says, and commit to a time that's just for you and your boo. Maybe you love preparing dinner or going to the gym together or rushing home to watch the latest episode of your favorite TV show while eating takeout from that place you went to for your first date? Whatever it is that consistently provides feel-good moments of connection for you, make that thing your standing date. After working crazy hours and caring for our child, we look forward to spending time together in the bed where we cuddle and pillow-talk before we fall asleep. We'll recap our days, talk about the baby, or watch television, but it's definitely our special time.

2. **Be intentional about establishing device-free time.** If your goal is to be in a relationship that goes the distance, you're going to have to put some distance between you and your phone. Not only is the device (and all the apps that come with it) a distraction, it hinders alone time, creates unnecessary friction, and often sparks feelings of competition. Listen to your partner if they say the phone is an issue, then offer to schedule blocks of time when you will not check emails, send texts, or post on social media. If adhering to a schedule is still too hard, you may have to follow in our footsteps and bring out the big guns—putting the phone in a lockbox with a timer. Don't make the mistake that we did and set the timer for twenty-six hours, otherwise you'll have to break the lock or go phone-free for a longer period of time.

Reflection

DaRealBBJudy

I'm a daddy's girl. From the time I brought a puppy home when my mother said I couldn't have one and Dad kept the secret, to the day he put me over his shoulder and tried to take me out of a bad relationship, our bond has always been strong. Even when I became a rebellious teenager who had her first child at fifteen and was put out of the house, my dad was still a phone call away.

I think about my dad a lot when I look at where my life is now. He was a hard worker and an entrepreneur. Whatever he wanted to do, he did it. I am a first-generation millionaire who built a company that has amassed millions. My company started out small and was built from the ground up. I sold products that I hand made from my beauty salon. Within two years I had outgrown my salon. By year four I purchased a forty-thousand-square-foot warehouse and scaled my business. Today, my company is worth more than one hundred million dollars.

I'm also in a beautiful marriage with a woman who supports and loves me unconditionally. I always imagined that my father would be the one to walk me down the aisle. But I didn't get married until I was forty. Who knew he wouldn't be here? I think he would be proud of who I have turned out to be. I got the recipe for love and success from him.

13 Perfectly Imperfect

After the initial excitement of your relationship has passed and the novelty of your amazing connection has worn off, you will discover that the person who makes your heart skip a beat when they smile or your toes curl in bed (yes, lawd!) has a bunch of flaws and imperfections that you never noticed before. The reaction is the same for everyone. First, it's shock and disbelief. Then comes disgust. You cannot believe this person you love enjoys eating pickled pig lips with potato chips and an Icee. No matter how much they say it's good, you can't get past the fact that they're eating this stuff that you think is nasty as fuck with the same mouth that they kiss you with. Can you say yuck? Better yet, don't come near me for at least a week.

Or maybe you discover your significant other likes to go to the bathroom with the door open and you can hear (and smell) them doing their business while you sit in disbelief. How could something that smells that bad come out of that person's body? And why are you just learning about these flaws of theirs now?

Well, the gag is: Everyone is on their best behavior in the beginning of a relationship. Of course, you want your boo to see all of your admirable qualities first. And as soon as you know neither of you is going anywhere, that's when the stranger things start to rear their annoying heads. One by one you start to notice things that make your right eye twitch, and you wonder if the *Invasion of the Body Snatchers* is a real thing because ain't no way this person in front of you who's been picking their damn nose for thirty minutes is the same person you fell for and sleep next to at night. Nope. Can't be.

But it is.

If you're in a relationship and things are getting serious, undoubtedly you've come face-to-face with your partner's unique little habits or eccentricities that disappoint, frustrate, or creep the hell out of you. How are you supposed to continue with them while their very existence feels like nails on a chalkboard at times?

It's not easy, but at some point in the relationship you must make a conscious choice to accept that merging your lives into one literally and figuratively involves accepting that it comes along with some junk.

GOLDEN RULE:

"EVERYBODY'S GOT THEIR SOMETHING. GET USED TO IT."

If you want to be in a relationship, you're gonna have to learn to accept each other's quirks because everyone has them. These little traits, whether physical, behavioral, or personality-driven, are what make us unique. While some quirks may be endearing, others can be more challenging to deal with. Or, to put it bluntly, they can be annoying or gross. But to build a lasting relationship, learning to adjust to or even celebrate your partner's eccentricities is key because it's a part of who they are. By accepting and understanding these idiosyncrasies, you and your partner can develop a deeper connection that's based on love, respect, and appreciation. Bad habits can be worked on, but trying to change your partner will be a losing battle. We are who we are, and it is important to value the distinctive qualities you each bring to the relationship. Learning to embrace differences can also bring a sense of humor and lightheartedness into your dynamic. Being able to laugh at each other's annoying quirks can add a little fun to how you interact. Ultimately, accepting each other's unique traits is a testament of your capability to love unconditionally. Love is never perfect, but being loved and accepted for who you are is what's ideal.

DaRealBBJudy: We really got to know and experience each other's quirks once I relocated to Atlanta and moved into the condo. *Beaurtiful* was staying with me so much I guess you can say we moved in with each other before we formally moved in. But spending all that time together gave us a chance to experience each other's behavior before we moved into our house. One of the things that became apparent once we got all of our things into one place is that we're both pack rats. We have two full closets upstairs. We have an extra closet room that has plenty of things in it. There's also two garages packed with *Beaurtiful*'s stuff. And she's got her things in closets in our extra rooms. I would dare say we are borderline hoarders because neither one of us likes to throw stuff away. *Beaurtiful* literally has boots from when Jesus walked the earth.

Da Brat: So I do have a couple pairs of shoes that have sentimental value. I might have bought them when I did my first record or something. I wouldn't say I'm a pack rat or hoarder. I do get rid of things. Before we moved into our house I gave away a lot of stuff to different churches and the less fortunate. I still have about thirty tubs of clothes in the garage that I haven't touched since we moved in, and there's a whole bunch of stuff that I need to sort through that I haven't gotten to yet, but I will. I'll probably just give all the things away or throw it all out because if I haven't used it in three or four years, I'm not going to use it.

There are some things that I feel I shouldn't get rid of because they're keepsakes that have sentimental value. There are also things I will need at some point. Like, when I travel to Chicago. My collection of jackets, coats, a few furs, leathers, and other winter stuff could be of use. Judy may think we are hoarders, but I disagree. If we were hoarders, we would have much more stuff than we do. But I will say this about my things . . . at least I have clothes in my closet that I actually wear more than once.

DaRealBBJudy: Despite what *Beaurtiful* thinks, I wear my clothes more than once. But stuff that's significant like my birthday dress that I was photographed in, I can't wear that again anytime soon, but I can wear it again at some point. All I'll say is that I purge my clothes more often than she does.

GOLDEN RULE:

"DON'T SHIT ON THE THINGS YOUR PARTNER ENJOYS."

The success and growth of your relationship will depend on both you and your partner feeling valued and respected, especially when it comes to your individual interests. Dismissing or invalidating each other's passions can lead to a whole host of issues. First, it can cause resentment in the partner who feels disregarded. Over time, they may start to believe you are uninterested in what they enjoy or, worse, that their interests don't matter to you. Invalidating your partner's passions might also make them feel as if they need to hide parts of who they are by hesitating to share their thoughts and feelings with you out of fear of being dismissed. To foster a healthy relationship environment, be open-minded and receptive to each other's viewpoints and interests, even if you don't share them. You don't have to develop a passion for everything your partner likes. But showing support by actively listening to them discuss their interests, and even asking questions, will do wonders in making your partner feel like they matter. At the same time, while respecting your partner's interests is important, so is being honest about your feelings. It's okay if you don't wish to participate in certain activities, and you shouldn't feel pressure to do so if it's truly not your thing. You don't have to do everything together for your relationship to work and be mutually beneficial. You both can be free to be yourselves and engage in activities you enjoy, even if it means you do them separately.

Da Brat: We have tried to throw away things together, but there is always something that we find that one of us thinks is valuable and the other doesn't. Like, my Weed Eater string. Our house is huge, and we hire people to help us maintain the property. Because I also enjoy doing yard work, I purchased my own blower and Weed Eater.

We were shooting our reality show while we were cleaning out the basement, and I found the string to my Weed Eater among the stuff. Judy didn't hesitate and told me to throw it away. I said no. It always seems like we fuss with each other every time the camera crew is around, and we got into it about the string. Judy didn't understand why I needed to keep it when someone else takes care of the weeds. My feelings were crushed. I trim weeds, cut our hedges, and do other stuff when our maintenance people aren't around. I was hurt and embarrassed. If I say I need something, then I need it. Also, just because she doesn't see me trimming weeds doesn't mean I'm not out there doing it. For all she knows, she could have been on the phone or something the last time I was out there with my Weed Eater. I might not do it a lot, but when I do I enjoy it. And, yes, I did keep the string.

GOLDEN RULE:

"TRY A LITTLE TENDERNESS."

By showing compassion and empathy toward each other, you and your significant other will be able to navigate your differences with grace and love. Tenderness creates space for vulnerability and honesty to flourish and can help you and your partner develop a deeper, more intimate connection. In moments of disagreement, approaching each other with tenderness can prevent arguments from escalating into the hurtful territory. A tender approach can help you usher in a more productive conversation so you're both able to hear and understand each other. Practicing tenderness isn't just about making sure your disagreements don't spiral into shouting matches. It's about making each other feel cherished, even in the ordinary moments. A gentle touch, a kind word of support, or even showing some patience when stress is running high can demonstrate that you are operating from a place of love and care. Tenderness serves as a powerful reminder that you and your partner are on the same team and will work toward a resolution rather than be each other's opposition.

Da Brat: My wife has a lip-picking habit that I can't stand because she really goes too far. If there's a dry patch on her lips, she'll bite the dry skin off and then she'll pick at her lips and start to peel the skin. She'll keep at it until eventually she'll go too far and the skin will be raw. There will be a little spot on her lips, and it'll look like her lips are hurting. It's truly an obsession for her. This thing with her lips worries me, but I also realized she's a picker. Don't let me or one of the kids have a dry skin moment or anything because she'll get the tweezers and she'll pick at it. For shits and giggles and to give her something to do, I will put Elmer's school glue on parts of my arm and leg where there isn't any hair and just let her go to town and pick the dried glue off in one piece. It's the weirdest thing, but she loves it.

When she starts picking at her lips, I have to get up and leave the room because I know it's something that she needs to do. If she feels there's something there, it'll bother her and she won't be happy until she picks the skin off. I'll opt to leave the room and give her time to pick her lips until she feels some sort of satisfaction because she's clearly stressed out about something. I just hate that she will peel too far, and it will cause her lip to bleed a little. I wish she could just stop, but it's a habit.

Although I hate that it's something she does, I do understand her need to do it because I used to smoke cigarettes and weed and drink Hennessy, which is my favorite. But I would never get wasted to the point where I would throw up. That happened when I was a teenager but not as an adult. Even though Judy wasn't bothered by me smoking weed or drinking alcohol, she did have an issue with the cigarettes.

GOLDEN RULE:

"DON'T NAG OR DEMAND."

As romantic partners trying to work through your differences, you should know that nagging and demanding are ineffective ways to communicate. Constant nagging or issuing demands can create an unpleasant and negative dynamic in your relationship, making it difficult for you and your significant other to engage in meaningful conversations or resolve your conflicts. The partner on the receiving end may become defensive and frustrated and may choose to tune out or shut down. When effective communication stops, the opportunity for understanding and a resolution is also over. Demanding behavior from a partner can also create a power struggle where one partner feels controlled or pressured by the other. This kind of imbalance erodes mutual respect and throws the relationship completely out of whack. If you reach an impasse on an issue impacting the relationship, the best approach is to find the middle ground. Rather than repeatedly pressing an issue or insisting something should only be done your way, focus on expressing your needs in a way that invites collaboration instead of resistance. One of the most effective ways to prevent nagging and demands from dominating how you and your partner relate to each other is to prioritize creating a safe and open environment where you both feel free to express yourselves. Instead of fixating on what your partner is or isn't doing, acknowledging their efforts, encouraging progress, and avoiding criticism will help you keep the peace.

DaRealBBJudy: I don't smoke. I don't drink. I don't do any of that stuff and never really have. Being a picker is my one vice—especially when my nerves are bad. But I don't like cigarettes, and I hated that *Beaurtiful* smoked. I did speak honestly with her that my kids' grandmother was a chronic smoker and died from it. She played an instrumental role in my children's lives, and we were all impacted by her death. I didn't think bullying *Beaurtiful* about her smoking would change the situation. Instead, I asked her to at least make it where she could stay with me as long as possible. I asked her not to take any years away from me. If she was going to smoke, at least smoke less. I didn't give a shit about her smoking weed or drinking. She had never been so inebriated that she became somebody different. And she'd never been so intoxicated that she didn't come home. So I didn't mind the drinking. But the cigarettes? I hated them.

GOLDEN RULE:

"SEE THE BIGGER PICTURE."

When you and your significant other are able to see the bigger picture in your relationship, it can help you work through your differences in a more constructive way. Keeping the bigger picture in mind allows you to focus on what truly matters rather than getting bogged down in the details of a disagreement. Instead of dwelling on who's right or wrong, taking a step back to understand each other's viewpoints can lead to a compromise. Seeing the bigger picture can also remind you why your love connection was sparked in the first place. This shift in perspective helps redirect attention away from the disagreement and back to what initially brought you together. Rather than allowing a conflict to drive a wedge between you, reconnecting with the foundation of your bond can help guide you toward a resolution instead of continued friction. When you both are focused on the bigger picture, such as maintaining a healthy relationship, it can help you stay committed to working through challenges rather than letting small disagreements derail your progress.

Da Brat: I tried to smoke away from Judy, but she could still smell it. So I began smoking less. When we moved in together I could only smoke in the studio. I cut back from a pack a day to half a pack a day. Then, from half a pack to about ten cigarettes a day. It took time for me to break the habit because a cigarette is good when you get up in the morning. It's also good when you're sitting on the toilet taking a shit. A cigarette is everything after you eat. It also goes well with some good Cognac. But once I stopped smoking cigarettes I realized I didn't need to drink. I was able to wean myself off, and once we decided we were trying to get pregnant, I was completely done.

The Takeaway

No matter how much in love we are, adjusting to a significant other's habits and quirks can be a challenging process that requires patience, understanding, and perhaps access to a she-shed for a little personal space every now and then. The choice to maintain the bond with your partner will require accepting each other for who you are, flaws and all. It's also important to be open to making changes in order to meet each other halfway. Here are a few more golden rules to help you lay the groundwork for a long-lasting and fulfilling relationship where your differences can unite you rather than drive you apart:

1. **Find the funny.** Laughter is a great stress reliever. You and your significant other's quirky habits may be great fodder for humorous moments together. Tread lightly, as you should really know your partner and their sense of humor well enough so they don't feel like the butt of your jokes.

2. **Talk about "the thing."** If your partner is doing something that drives you absolutely crazy, it is your duty to let them know. Instead of becoming angry or frustrated, verbalize how their behavior makes you feel. Of course, you should wait until you're calm and in a decent mood to keep tempers from flaring.

3. **Do a self check-in.** Is it really your partner's actions that are triggering you, or are you upset about something else? Take an inventory of your feelings before approaching them. If you're really mad or frustrated about something else, it's not fair to blame your partner for those emotions.

14 Business Acumen/ Financial Goals

There's a popular adage that is often used as cautionary advice for entrepreneurs. It's said that most business owners don't plan to fail, they fail to plan. We believe the same is true for relationships. Most couples don't plan for their relationship to fail, they simply fail to plan for their union to succeed. Of course, all the world will tell you that a huge stumbling block for couples is money. Most of the time it's because we choose partners without doing all the necessary due diligence. We make sure we ask the basic questions like marital/dating status, children, and employment, but the topic of money and finances gets danced around, if mentioned at all.

First of all, talking about money is uncomfortable. It doesn't matter who you are. But it's even more uncomfortable for those who don't have any. Our theory on why conversations about money are especially difficult for women is that they fear they will be seen as gold diggers.

Side note: Isn't it funny how that label is primarily put on women? You might think the gold digger label is solely an issue in heterosexual relationships. FYI: It's not.

Sexual orientation be damned, anyone who's in the market for a significant other or who's already in a relationship is wary of getting involved with someone who brings little to the table and can eat you out of house and home. Hell, if you're not supercareful, these types of folks just might take your table, too.

Everyone wants to be loved for who they are and not for what they have or can potentially make. But when it comes to deciding whether someone may or may not be a suitable mate, a lot of us opt to pursue a love connection without knowing whether the person they are in a relationship with has different financial goals (if any at all), unhealthy spending habits, or, worse, a whole lot of unpaid debt.

GOLDEN RULE:

"RUN YOUR RELATIONSHIP LIKE A BUSINESS."

Running a relationship like a business can lead to success for several reasons. Just as businesses thrive when there's a strategy and clear direction in place, your relationship can also benefit from a well-thought-out plan that realistically defines desired outcomes and outlines your shared commitment to achieve them. Since many businesses track performance metrics, there's no reason you and your boo shouldn't do the same. Frequent, honest dialogues to check in on feelings, discuss finances, set goals, and adjust responsibilities can prevent the relationship from drifting into an unfulfilling space. A clear intention to monitor your individual and collective well-being ensures that the love between you and your partner continues to flow steadily. Still, a relationship is not a business, so striking the right balance between structure and spontaneity is key. A mix of fun, affection, and thoughtful planning can keep things from feeling too rigid or controlled. By approaching your relationship with the same level of care and dedication as you would a business, you set the tone for communication, teamwork, and mutual respect to serve as guideposts that help your partnership to grow while meeting both your needs.

Because we are two women who have achieved a certain level of professional and financial success, the decision to get married and merge our lives meant we were also merging businesses. While the love we have for each other was (and is) the primary reason why we chose each other, with any merger the financial health of both parties is essential in order to position the relationship for long-term success. For us, it meant having an honest conversation about what we were each bringing to the relationship so we could establish a firm foundation on which to build our new life together.

Da Brat: My aunt and I grew up together in the same household. We were my grandmother's favorites. She was my grandmother's favorite daughter, and I was my grandmother's favorite grandchild. When my music career took off and I became rich and famous at a young age, I had no idea how to manage my money. Luckily, my aunt whom I love and trust has a tax firm that specializes in finances. As I grew up in the industry, she watched my money and made sure things were taken care of. I have never in my whole entire life had to budget because my aunt has been my accountant, business manager, keeper, and doer of all of my things my entire career. Once Judy came into my life I suddenly had to think about how things were set up because we were talking a lot about marriage, and there was so much about my own financial situation that I didn't know.

DaRealBBJudy: When we got into our relationship, one of the first big hurdles we had to clear was how we were going to manage our money. *Beaurtiful* explained to me how her aunt took care of everything for her, but since we were planning on taking a huge step in our relationship, I felt it was necessary that any conversations I needed to have about *Beaurtiful*'s money should be had with her. I didn't want to talk to anyone else. So I asked her what she planned on doing about her money management situation because as her future wife I didn't want to make decisions about money with anyone who wasn't her. I felt strongly that as a person who doesn't like to ask for anything, if I ever had to ask her for anything, going through a third party was unacceptable to me. It had to be she and I talking about money and making decisions together.

GOLDEN RULE:

"GET YOUR FINANCIAL DUCKS IN ORDER."

The management of your individual and collective finances can make or break your relationship. Even for those who simply "go together" and haven't ventured into cohabitation, financial (mis) management can be a key predictor of whether a relationship will be sustainable. Money problems aren't just about what is (or isn't) in your bank account. They can interfere with your ability to pay the bills, maintain a social life, care for loved ones, and plan for the future. Being financially aligned with your partner is a huge advantage. When one or both partners don't have their financial ducks in order, it can lead to stress, resentment, and conflict. Transparency about your expenses, spending habits, and long-term financial goals allows you and your partner to make informed decisions on how to work together to enjoy life without financial hardship looming overhead. Whether you decide to merge finances, split expenses, or maintain separate accounts, the critical step is having an honest discussion about your status. Working together to pay down debt, save money, and maintain financial stability puts you on the path to building a relationship that's not only emotionally strong but financially secure as well.

Da Brat: It took some time, but I had to start learning how to manage my shit immediately. It had been more than twenty years, and I was trying to look at bank accounts and understand what everything meant. During the course of my career, whenever there were deals and things happening, I would look over stuff before signing documents, but I was suddenly in a position where I not only had to know how my finances were set up, but also how much I actually had. Things got even more complicated because at the same time I was in the middle of a tense legal situation. As mentioned earlier, I had spent time in prison for this matter, but I was also being sued. I was planning to keep up the fight, but the situation was taking a toll on our relationship and our future plans. Though I didn't want Judy to get involved, she was insistent on us working together to resolve the lawsuit so we could close out this frustrating period of my life and move forward with our plans to start anew as a married couple.

GOLDEN RULE:

"BE HONEST ABOUT WHERE THE MONEY RESIDES."

When you and your significant other are open and honest about your individual financial situations, it'll position you to be able to work together to create a budget and set financial goals that are realistic and achievable. The more transparent you are about your money, the more you can prevent arguments and misunderstandings, which are common sources of conflict in relationships. By having these conversations early on and revisiting them regularly, you and your significant other can build a solid foundation for your financial future while strengthening your relationship in the process. But financial honesty isn't just about the numbers. It's about discussing spending habits, values, and any struggles you may have with money. Being partners means recognizing how your approach to money can affect your relationship as a whole. If you're bogged down in debt, a spendthrift, debt-free, or a chronic saver, these are important details that you and your partner should share and understand. Your financial tendencies don't have to be deal-breakers, but they should help you and your partner determine how to move forward. Knowing where your money goes can help determine whether it's best to manage finances together or support each other's individual efforts to maintain or establish stability. Financial honesty is an investment in your relationship. Understanding what you both have, how you manage it, and what your goals are can help you prevent financial instability from undermining your connection.

DaRealBBJudy: As a part of the resolution of *Beaurtiful*'s legal dispute, we negotiated that we would put some money down and then pay a certain amount to the other party every month. But before we could move forward we had to figure out how we were going to manage the financial liability by looking closely at the numbers. Managing money is an area that I excel in, so I needed to know what we were working with to determine the amount that we could put down and how much we could reasonably afford as a payment each month.

Getting to the answers took us some time because *Beaurtiful* still had to consult with her aunt. It wasn't that she didn't know anything at all about her money, but her income sources were multilayered. There was money from her TV and radio cohosting gigs, performances, music royalties, and other residuals. With a multitude of sources to tally up, we sat down with her aunt and my accountants to figure out the sum of all the parts and finally took care of this situation that had been bugging us both.

• • •

A relationship, just like a business, needs to have individuals in charge of the areas of their expertise. No entrepreneur in their right mind would put a social media manager at the helm of the accounting department. It just doesn't make sense. To prevent unnecessary conflicts and other complications in our relationship, when it comes to our money, the same rules apply as in determining who leads and who follows—we each take the lead in the areas where we are the strongest.

DaRealBBJudy: Once I took the big step to relocate to Atlanta from New Orleans, the next item on the agenda was merging homes. The decision to buy a huge house that sits on six acres of land was the second significant financial decision we made together. The first being resolving her legal conflict. Neither one of us had ever experienced living in a house so large. Our first priority was to figure out the lay of the land . . . literally. With expenses including two water bills, two light bills, yard and pool crews, and maintenance people, we tap into our individual strengths to make sure the house and our finances run smoothly.

GOLDEN RULE:

"FIND WAYS TO INCREASE YOUR EARNING POTENTIAL TOGETHER."

Generating additional income will open up new opportunities for you and your significant other to invest in your future together. You may have dreams of buying a house, starting a family, or taking a nice, long vacation abroad. Finding new ways to finance your plans will make it easier for them to become a reality sooner than later. Increasing your earning potential doesn't always mean taking on another job or two, but it shouldn't be out of the question. Side hustles and strategic investing are great ways to increase your individual and collective earning potential. Boosting your income can also be achieved by expanding your skill set, obtaining a degree, or pursuing certifications that make you a stronger candidate for a promotion or a higher-paying position. Whatever path you and your boo choose, pooling resources and working together to increase your financial worth can help you improve your lifestyle together or achieve the goals you've outlined for yourselves and the relationship. Even if financial stability is your primary goal so the bills don't keep you from enjoying your lives as a couple, a collaborative approach to wealth building ensures that financial growth is a shared responsibility and priority that benefits the future of your relationship.

DaRealBBJudy: Keeping our physical and financial houses in order is vitally important for us to maintain the healthy status of our relationship. Having solid ground beneath us put us in a position to pursue and land the amazing opportunity that our TV show, *Brat Loves Judy*, offers us in the way of increasing our earning potential, growing our audience, and being ambassadors for LGBTQIA+ relationships.

Da Brat: I was doing *Growing Up Hip Hop Atlanta*, which starred Jermaine Dupri and his daughter as well as other celebrity kids whose parents were hip-hop stars. When my relationship with Judy started, I was finally in my truth. My baby came on the show with me, and the team from the production company was really drawn to how much we loved each other and how different I had become from meeting the love of my life. We agreed to do our show because it was an opportunity for people to see how we relate to each other, all the things we go through, and how we resolve issues. We felt it was important for the public to see two Black women who are successful professionally love each other and live a great life together.

DaRealBBJudy: Since we let each other take the lead in the areas where we are the strongest, *Beaurtiful* was the one who negotiated a deal for us that was absolutely crazy. She made sure that the financials for my deal were top notch. As someone who is very new to TV, the amount that she secured for me was unheard of. She also made sure we have final say on edits. That, too, is unreal but it was all due to her. Her negotiation skills put us in the position for Kaleidoscope to have a lot of visibility, which has had a tremendous impact on the company's growth.

Beaurtiful also made sure the people in our camp who regularly appear on the show are taken care of. In reality television, if you're not well-known, you really don't get paid. But *Beaurtiful* advocated not just for me, but for all our people so they also get to walk away with decent checks. The show is essentially about us and has increased our earning potential together, but it's become bigger than that because it also provides a financial blessing to others.

The Takeaway

Money problems are a typical source of tension in relationships, and ignoring them may have far-reaching consequences. When it comes to how you and your significant other should handle your finances within your relationship, there is no standard that works perfectly for everyone. Here are a few more golden rules that can assist you and your partner with crafting a financial strategy that is most suitable to your situation:

1. **Put all the cards on the table.** Before anything else, an honest conversation must be had where you discuss how much money you both are working with, your personal beliefs around money, and your financial objectives. This will give you a clear idea of what your financial situation is and how you will work together to reach your collective goals. This is also the time to have a conversation about spending habits and whether bills are current. You both must be willing to come clean about everything without judgment. The money conversation must be

a safe space, otherwise it will always be difficult to talk about and get a handle on your financial goals. If paying off debt is a struggle, talk about where the roadblocks are. Perhaps you'll be able to hold each other accountable in making sure the debt gets paid down before you move forward with adding other large purchases or costs? Be sure to also talk about how you deal with money. A spender or risk-taker may eventually butt heads with a frugal person or chronic saver. Being forthright about your financial situation from the start will give you tremendous insight and help you work together to fix any problems and make the most of future opportunities.

2. **Talk about money regularly.** Your money conversation shouldn't be a one-off. You're not going to be able to do a one and done here. No ma'am. No sir. Your money talks must be ongoing. Be sure to check in with your partner on a regular basis and discuss your views and financial progress. Whether you want to admit it or not, you both will bring money habits into the relationship that can result in you bumping heads. By having regular conversations about money, it'll become easier to understand where there are roadblocks so you can get around them without driving each other crazy.

3. **Know your worth. Literally.** Examine all of your financial documents including bank and savings account statements, pay stubs, credit card statements, investment reports, etc. Keep in mind this isn't information that you want to share with someone you just started shacking up with. This should only be done

with someone you're serious about. Even if you opt not to share all the details of your worth with your partner at this time, at least do this on your own to gauge your financial health. If you're doing it together, remember money and money management are sensitive topics to some people. Refrain from making any snide comments about that negative balance in their checking account. Being part of a team means you are willing to accept the good, bad, and frequently overdrawn.

4. **Create a budget.** Whatever your financial goals are with your partner, a budget will be your road map. Without a budget it will leave too much of an opportunity for things to go awry. A budget is your accountability partner. It's also not a one-off either. Put a monthly, bimonthly, or even quarterly appointment date on the calendar where you and your partner evaluate the budget to see how things are going, identify areas for improvement, and make any necessary revisions.

5. **Set short- and long-term goals.** You'll need to have clear objectives for what you want to achieve. Are you thinking about making a house purchase? Do you want to take some fabulous vacations? You may put that extra money toward your shared objectives if, after creating a budget, you still have enough left over.

6. **Test the waters.** If you're not living together and you want to see how you work together with the management of money, consider doing a trial run before pooling all of your money together. Try opening up a joint account with a specific goal like investing,

saving money, creating a vacation fund, or even just paying bills. With a trial run you'll be able to see how you and your partner work together on a common financial goal.

DaRealBBJudy: I was in a previous relationship with someone who had a gambling problem. We were also in different tax brackets. We decided to take a certain percentage of our income and put it into a pot to pay bills. We each put in 30 percent of our income, but the amount it came to for me was different because I made more money and I also came with three children. But I made sure my obligation went into the pot no matter what. I was perfectly fine with putting in 30 percent because those were my children. I also didn't want to change my current lifestyle. I did not want to downgrade because my partner at the time could not afford to pay half of what they had never paid before. The 30 percent also made sure my former partner prioritized their contribution since there was a gambling issue.

7. **Don't be deceitful.** If you and your partner have committed to pooling your financial resources, don't do things behind each other's back like keeping a secret account or adding more credit cards. If you're working toward a mutual financial objective, keep everything on the up-and-up. So no hidden Amazon purchases with that "mad money" account or credit card your mama told you to have "just in case." You may decide together that you both can have small individual accounts for odds and ends or gifts, but for the sake of the relationship, make sure it's a part of the rules ahead of time. Finding out that someone is hiding money is a huge red flag.

15 Keeping God First

We've shared so many of the principles that have helped us navigate the ups and downs of this thing called love. While we are comfortable telling the world we are two lesbian women who fell in love, it's important to note that there's one key distinction. We are two God-fearing women before we are anything else.

Our personal relationships with God are at the root of everything we do as individuals and as a couple. With God as our foundation it has enabled us to build our relationship on shared values and beliefs. We ultimately feel more connected to each other because believing in God is a shared language that shapes our interactions with each other, guides our decisions, helps us overcome obstacles, and keeps us grounded in what's most important—loving each other and strengthening our bond. We are not perfect, but we are perfect for each other, and we believe it's God's influence in our lives that has enabled our relationship to flourish.

GOLDEN RULE:

"A SPIRITUAL CONNECTION MUST BE WHAT CONNECTS YOU."

Sharing a spiritual connection with your significant other is one of the most beautiful ways to develop a relationship. Finding your partner attractive and sharing common interests help open the door to discovering true compatibility. But when you're both operating from a shared belief system that guides your morals, defines your values, and shapes your actions, pursuing the relationship can seem even more purposeful because you have something important in common. While opposites definitely attract, having a spiritual foundation in common is an indication that you and your partner live by very similar, if not the same, core principles. As you and your significant other grow in your relationship, your shared spiritual connection provides even more opportunities to bond, like praying and attending church together. Being spiritually aligned doesn't mean you won't argue or have difficult times. However, your shared faith can ensure that bridging the gap between differing beliefs or worldviews won't be as big of a challenge as it may be for other couples. The trust you have in a Higher Power makes it easier for you and your partner to build something together that extends beyond romance and attraction. In each other you'll have a spiritual partner who not only supports your journey but also has their own commitment to maintaining their faith.

Da Brat: Nothing about my relationship and marriage to Judy is "traditional." But this is our life. Our story. Our journey. Our connection to the church and God has molded us. It also shapes our relationship. I was taught to pray for everything. As a couple, our belief in God and prayer is a part of everything we do. We pray when we get in the car to keep us safe. We pray over our food. We pray together before I perform. There's no way that we are blessed the way we are blessed and God is not responsible for it.

DaRealBBJudy: *Beaurtiful* always speaks about growing up in a sanctified church and how the practices are different from other churches, but we have the same beliefs in the power of God and the importance of putting God first in our lives. I was raised Catholic, but I converted to be a Baptist at the age of sixteen. My mom was Baptist, and my father was Catholic. They went to two separate churches and had two different sets of faith, but they both believed in God. My parents gave my siblings and me the right to choose where we wanted to land. They let us decide which side of the fence we wanted to be on. I went to my mom's church because I felt I related more to that experience. Catholicism is a lot of discipline and ritual type of stuff. You stand up, you kneel down, and you pray. Nothing is wrong with that, but at the time when going to my mama's church, I would listen to the Word and it would resonate a little bit more with me than what I was hearing at that Catholic church. So I converted.

Beaurtiful and I know that we're being judged and some think that, based on their outlook in life and what they feel the Bible says, our love is not acceptable. But we wholeheartedly know that God is in our relationship and that our marriage is blessed.

Da Brat: People have been talking about me since the '90s when I entered the rap game. I was young, but as I matured and started to discover my sexuality, everyone was always curious and felt like they knew I was gay even before I did. In the beginning it hurt. But after being in the industry for years, you realize no matter what you do, you're not going to be able to please everybody. My mom is still sanctified and Judy's mom preaches and is active in the church, but they don't judge us. They love us for who we are and don't make us feel bad even if they don't agree with our lifestyle. They love us as their children. They have seen what we have gone through in different relationships. Some of those other relationships were with the opposite sex and were not as positive or loving as they should have been. But now they see their children happy. I'm grateful to God that our families are there for us. I'm sure if I go back to my granny's church, some of the older saints won't be too happy with my marriage to Judy, but I can't worry about that. I have to worry about myself. And for a long time, I lived my life worried about being judged and not my own happiness. I am grateful that our families love us. And we know God loves us, too.

GOLDEN RULE:

"YOUR FAITH MUST BE BIGGER THAN YOUR CHALLENGES."

Your relationship will be tested. You and your significant other may, at some point, question whether you should stay together or go your separate ways. But if you're both grounded in a belief in God, then your faith can become a powerful resource.

> Faith won't guarantee that you'll be free from struggles, but it should give you the courage and confidence so that when they do appear, you're able to face them without fear. Your faith exists to remind you that difficulties are merely temporary, and with patience, perseverance, and prayer (hallelujah!), you and your partner can make it through anything. A relationship that's built on faith can thrive not because it will be free of struggle, but because it's strengthened by the belief that with God anything and everything is possible.

DaRealBBJudy: I am grateful that things have changed over time. My mother may not have understood initially, but now she sees that I'm in a loving relationship. She looks at us and sees happiness. She looks at our relationship for what it is versus who we are or our gender.

But support wasn't always there for us, especially since the birth of our son. Initially, when people would say stuff about True, it bothered me a lot because he is an innocent child. Mothers always want to protect their children. Our choosing to have a child together and raising him in the limelight is controversial. I wholeheartedly believe, no matter the gender, that raising a child in love is the most important thing. Having a baby daddy isn't a guarantee to make a situation better just because it's a man and a woman. Our son is completely loved. And he will not miss anything.

Beaurtiful and I trust in God and we trust in each other. Our daily focus is to home in on each other and our relationship because we can't convince people to accept us, who we are, and what we're doing. The outside chatter is bothersome, but we have a home where God is at the center of our lives. And we also have a wonderful church home where our spirits get fed regularly.

I met William Murphy, the bishop of our church, when I was living in New Orleans. He had come to the church I was going to at the time, and was a guest speaker. I met him in passing. After a traumatic experience happened in my life, Bishop Murphy reached out to me. From there I started watching and attending his church because I felt connected to him through music. In addition to being a pastor, Bishop Murphy is an awesome gospel singer. I also love his preaching style. He teaches in the way that I speak, and he speaks in a way that I am able to hear and understand what he's saying. He's very relatable. He's also completely different from what I was exposed to, having been raised in the Catholic church. It feels great to have someone be able to break the Word of the Lord down so you can comprehend it. It's also wonderful to belong to a congregation where you are able to come as you are. Bishop Murphy has never judged *Beaurtiful* and me or our relationship. He's only tried to support us on our faith journey. He makes sure that we maintain a relationship with God and gives us the information we need in order to continue our walk with God.

Da Brat: I used to listen to Bishop Murphy's music all the time. I love his voice, and I love his singing. I didn't even know he preached. When we purchased our house and he came to bless it, that's when I realized he was the same person whose music I loved to listen to. The first couple of times that Judy and I went to his church, I would just cry. The atmosphere reminded me of when I used to go to church with my grandmother. It was the same feeling, and it made me miss my roots. Bishop Murphy's way of preaching the Word also resonated with me. It wasn't just good. It was positive. He knows how to make you feel special, and he knows how to communicate that you are special to God and you don't have to be a certain way. Bishop Murphy reminds us that as long as our hearts love God, that is the most important thing.

Another thing I love about attending Bishop Murphy's church is that there are so many young people and people who look like us in his church. Some of them wear sneakers. It's not like you ever have to be dressed a certain way in order to feel welcomed. Going to Bishop Murphy's church makes me feel like I'm at home.

DaRealBBJudy: A lot of people think they have to be perfect to show up to church, which is why they don't attend. But God wants you to come as you are. And we're able to be who we are at Bishop Murphy's church. I'm not judged or pressured to change who I am, how I speak, or what I do. Even though we have a relationship with Bishop Murphy outside of the church, we continue to fellowship with him and his congregation because we are able to get the Word from him and feel okay about who we are.

The Takeaway

In a relationship, putting God first means placing your faith and your spiritual connection with God at the forefront of your priorities as a couple. It involves integrating your views, values, and principles into your relationship and enabling them to impact your interactions and choices. Here are a few more golden rules to help you maintain your faith walk as you and your partner work toward building or maintaining a healthy, long-lasting relationship:

1. **Find a church home.** Attending church together is an excellent way to deepen your spiritual connection. Having a church community can offer you and your significant other emotional and social support throughout the stages of your relationship journey. If you're preparing for marriage or are in a marriage already, church counseling services or group meetings can connect you with other couples who share your beliefs and who may have helpful insight on working through difficult situations.

2. **Integrate prayer into everything you do.** There is no better way to see God's love at work in your life and your relationship than through prayer. It is the conduit through which God speaks to you, provides guidance, and reminds you of His undying love. Praying for and with your partner ensures that, beyond love and companionship, your relationship is grounded in a shared belief that God is at the center of both your lives and your relationship.

Reflection

DaRealBBJudy

My dad really spoiled me to death. But his love for me brought me to where I am now. In all my relationships, all I ever wanted was the kind of love that he showed me. To me, love makes you feel special: You're thought about, and you feel seen and heard. I always wanted that feeling that I was important to someone and I was their priority.

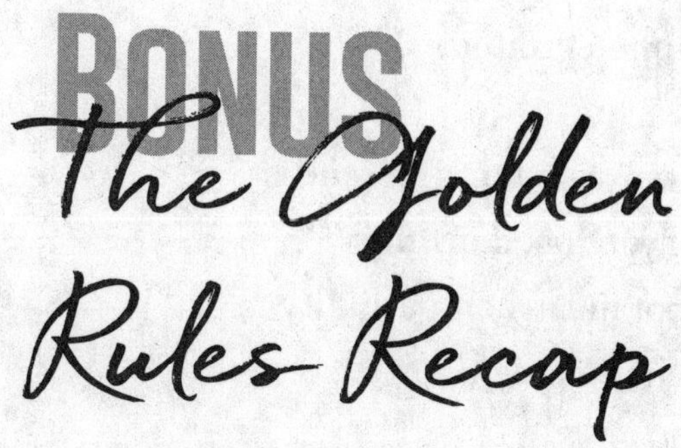

1. **The Golden Rules for Communication in a Relationship**

    - Determine the source of the communication breakdown.
    - Establish boundaries.
    - Take personal ownership of your role in the problem.
    - Accept the consequences.
    - Be honest about what's going on.
    - Check your motherfucking tone.
    - Be mindful of your body language.
    - Practice empathy and compassion.
    - Tune in.
    - Don't criticize and place blame.
    - Apologize.

2. The Golden Rules for Compatibility in a Relationship

- Determine your deal-breakers.
- Seek areas of common ground.
- Be flexible.
- Find an appreciation for your differences.
- It's okay to split if you just don't fit.
- Chemistry does not mean compatibility.
- Your authentic self is enough.

3. The Golden Rules for Fighting Fair in a Relationship

- Pinpoint why you're mad.
- Set the rules of the relationship.
- Try to understand each other's perspective.
- Take a time-out if necessary.
- Don't take your frustration out on each other.
- Don't go to bed angry.
- Stick to the issue.
- Pay attention to your own tendencies.
- Revisit the rules.
- Take off your armor.
- Stay away from the insults.
- Don't be passive-aggressive.
- Don't yell and talk over each other.
- Keep your hands to yourself.

4. **The Golden Rules for Building Trust in a Relationship**

- There is no vulnerability without trust.
- Take a risk together.
- Be supportive.
- Be honest. Own your truth.
- Set firm boundaries.
- Trust is earned.
- Read the tea leaves.
- Trust your gut.
- Be ready for war.

5. **The Golden Rules for Respect in a Relationship**

- Support each other's decisions.
- Listen to each other.
- Take responsibility.
- Keep the lines of communication open.
- Understand your partner's dos and don'ts.
- Find the compromise.
- Be loyal.
- Show some love.

6. **The Golden Rules for Sexual Chemistry in a Relationship**

- Be open to love.
- Go after what you want.
- Get your flirt on.

- Savor the slow burn.
- Sexual intimacy must be a priority.
- Get physical.
- Ask for feedback.
- Don't be selfish.
- Determine the rules of engagement.

7. **The Golden Rules for Leading/Following in a Relationship**

    - Set the house rules.
    - Accept an offer for help.
    - Determine the desired outcome.
    - Push your ego aside.
    - Create balance.

8. **The Golden Rules for Self-Love in a Relationship**

    - Self-criticism is counterproductive.
    - Find a safe and nonjudgmental space like counseling or therapy to explore your issues.
    - Take pride in your accomplishments.
    - Practice gratitude.
    - Make choices that feel right to you.
    - Let your creative energy flow.
    - Have your own damn thing.
    - Embrace optimism.
    - Get some sleep.
    - Reclaim your time.

9. **The Golden Rules for Prioritizing Each Other in a Relationship**

    - Make a big impression.
    - Be grateful for second chances.
    - Prioritize being friends.
    - Don't be afraid to risk embarrassment.
    - Be direct. Tell your partner what you want.
    - Take action.
    - Lead with love.

10. **The Golden Rules for Growing Together in a Relationship**

    - Allow the relationship to chart its own course.
    - Make sure you're on the same page.
    - Be open to new possibilities.
    - Don't get discouraged.
    - Check in with each other.
    - Let resilience become your superpower.
    - Always be willing to collaborate.

11. **The Golden Rules for the Pursuit of Happiness in a Relationship**

    - Define your needs.
    - Nurture to be nurtured.
    - Show appreciation for all things large and small.
    - Understand whom you're in a relationship with.

- Don't let small issues become big issues.
- Make your time together a good time.
- Be authentic.
- Share your truth.
- Discover love languages.
- Utilize what you know.

12. The Golden Rules for How to Never Stop Dating in a Relationship

- Be honest about the challenges.
- Figure out what works.
- Make them feel special.
- Catch them by surprise.
- Turn the intimacy up.
- Decide your "special" time.
- Be intentional about establishing device-free time.

13. The Golden Rules for Being Perfectly Imperfect in a Relationship

- Everybody's got their something. Get used to it.
- Don't shit on the things your partner enjoys.
- Try a little tenderness.
- Don't nag or demand.
- See the bigger picture.
- Find the funny.

- Talk about "the thing."
- Do a self check-in.

14. The Golden Rules for Business Acumen / Financial Goals in a Relationship

- Run your relationship like a business.
- Get your financial ducks in order.
- Be honest about where the money resides.
- Find ways to increase your earning potential together.
- Put all the cards on the table.
- Talk about money regularly.
- Know your worth. Literally.
- Create a budget.
- Set short- and long-term goals.
- Test the waters.
- Don't be deceitful.

15. The Golden Rules for Keeping God First in Your Relationship

- A spiritual connection must be what connects you.
- Your faith must be bigger than your challenges.
- Find a church home.
- Integrate prayer into everything you do.

Acknowledgments

Jesseca "Judy" Harris-DuPart

Whewwwww chile . . . where do I even begin? Writing this book was not on my bingo card, but most of the things in my life that are super great also weren't. I want to personally thank a few people who helped in some way or another.

First and foremost, I'd like to thank both of my parents. My dad was my inspiration for all of my entrepreneurial endeavors. I hope he's proud of me up there in heaven. My mom showed me what a supportive wife looks like, and I'm grateful I had the chance to witness a healthy relationship growing up. Mom, you are the reason I put God first. You instilled faith in me throughout my life, and I love you so much.

To my kids Deja, Byron Jr., Jordan, and True . . . I love you beyond words. Deja, I'm so proud of the mother you've become. Byron Jr., seeing you become a responsible adult lets me know that what I tried to teach y'all didn't go in one ear and out the other. Jordan, you have such a generous spirit, and I hope you'll always remember to look out for yourself, too. And to True, Momma is soooo proud to have you as mine. It's a blessing every day to get to love you.

To my small but mighty friend tribe, I appreciate everything y'all do, from providing listening ears to serving as prayer warriors. You're solution driven but still willing to sit with me in the problem, and you never take it to any other soul to share what isn't yours to share. Thank you for always having my back, supporting our marriage, and showing up for us in every way.

To the one that always makes sure no matter how many times I fall that I continue to get up. The man above. God, I appreciate you being there in my quiet storms and always protecting me even when I don't even know there's danger ahead. By trusting in you, I've learned to lean into faith instead of fear and confusion.

To my cosmetology teacher Mrs. Richardson, thank you for who you were to me at a time when I was lost and didn't even know myself. Thanks for pushing me to continue to pursue cosmetology even while pregnant. And thanks for giving me an opportunity to complete the program even after graduation. I appreciate you so much.

To my KHP family, who are more like family than staff. I love and appreciate y'all. Your creativity, loyalty, and dedication to helping the company grow means so much to me. I am grateful to have a team who believe in and trust in my vision. Thank you.

To our ONE-OF-A-KIND community, whether you wanna refer to yourselves as supporters, our social followers, fans, or KHP VIPs—without the continued support of so many of y'all around the world none of this would have been possible. We appreciate y'all and consider you family. It's our hope that our journey and transparency can keep y'all motivated, entertained, and hopeful. We love you.

Lastly, I wanna thank my BEAURTIFUL for showing me what love really means—a type of unconditional love that I've never seen (not even in movies). I love you past the moon and I am so blessed to be able to call you mines. (Yes with an "s.") Spending forever with you has made me the luckiest girl in the world. Thank you for not turning me down when I said I was interested in you 😊 😊. You're not only a blessing to me but to everyone you encounter and I love you so much for that.

Shawntae "Da Brat" Harris-DuPart

I would like to thank GOD for my very existence. HE continuously blesses me, looks beyond my faults and provides for my needs. Even when I don't understand, HE has a purpose for EVERYTHING and HE is always there to catch me when I fall and pull me right back up to where HE needs me to be.

My amazing mommie, who has been my prayer warrior, friend, and the best GanGan to my son EVER.

My Ainey Gail, who has been my protector and guardian of my bread my whole life. My godmother Debbie, BFF Stef, sister Dawn, and BFF Nicole Simpson . . . I speak to you guys more than anyone about everything and I appreciate our conversations.

My aunt and uncle Twig and Boopie (Polk), love u both. Punk, thank you for always being there for me as I grew into a woman. JD, thank you for believing in me, being my mentor and molding me to become the first solo female rapper to ever go platinum.

Thank you Bella, Lucy, and Nick Roses for always keeping my life, schedule, and business affairs in order. Thank you to my *Rickey Smiley Morning Show*, *Dish Nation*, and Kaleidoscope families.

To my li'l bros Mr. Rdot, Flick, Kito, my cuz Jeff, Big Al, Montana, Bow Wizzle, and so many more.

There are way too many of y'all to list but thank y'all for always having my back when I need you.

To my heart, soul, twin flame and everything in between . . . My BeauRtiful. When I wasn't even looking, you suddenly appeared and swept me clean off my feet. The way you love, protect, inspire, and motivate me to bet on myself is the best gift I could have ever received. Your heart is something I've never experienced. You are the sweetest and most thoughtful wife. No one in the world loves me like you do. I appreciate when you're tough on me and give me room to adjust and grow. Thank you for your patience. Your attention to detail and creativity is genius, baby. Your love language melts my heart every single day. You are absolutely what my life needed. I am so proud and grateful to be yours. I love you.

From the both of us . . .

This book would not have come to life without our incredible literary agent and partner, Ashley Coleman, and the Europa content team. Thank you for recognizing that *Brat Loves Judy* was just the beginning and that we had more of our story to tell. A heartfelt thank you to our brilliant editor, Patrik Henry Bass, and the Amistad team for believing in this book and its message.

We are especially grateful to Diane R. Paylor. Thank you for making us feel safe enough to share the things we once feared revealing, and helping us put the words on the page.

About the Authors

Jesseca Harris-Dupart, better known as "Judy," is a trailblazer in both the business and entertainment world and hails from the dynamic city of New Orleans. She is the CEO and founder of Kaleidoscope Hair Products. Harris-Dupart's innovative spirit led to the creation of the UniKorn collection, a hair line that specializes in anti-breakage, catering to the needs of those who frequently change their hairstyles. Her business acumen extends beyond the beauty industry as an influential social media and television personality and real estate investor.

She stars in We TV's *Brat Loves Judy*, alongside her partner, rapper Da Brat. Notable for its representation of an LGBTQ+ couple on reality TV, the show delves into their personal and professional lives, offering a unique glimpse into the dynamics of their relationship and careers.

Harris-Dupart's media appearances extend beyond her reality show. She has been featured in *Forbes*, *Essence*, *Black Enterprise*, *People*, and on *E!* and *BET*. Discussing her powerful journey to success, she shares the complexities of balancing business, love, and family, which resonates with many entrepreneurs who face similar challenges. She also provides valuable guidance and business insights by advising others to prioritize trust and have unwavering authenticity. She donated 20,000 units of Kaleidoscope's bestselling hair products at Harlem Pride in 2022 to underserved and marginalized members of the community around New York City. Her commitment to community service is deeply rooted, driven by a desire to leave a positive impact and support others.

Shawntae "Da Brat" Harris-DuPart—born in Chicago, Illinois, and better known by her stage name, Da Brat—is an American rap artist, profound writer, television and radio personality, actress, and executive music and television producer. Harris attended Kenwood Academy High School and the Academy of Scholastic Achievement, where she played seven different instruments in band. Da Brat's debut album, *Funkdafied*, was released in 1994 and entered the rap albums chart at number 1. The album went platinum, making her the first female solo rapper to sell one million units. The eponymous single reached number 1 on the rap singles chart and number 6 on the Billboard Hot 100, with her follow-up hit, "Give It 2 You," reaching number 26 on the Billboard Hot 100.

Da Brat has released four studio albums to date: *Funkdafied*, *Unrestricted*, *Anuthatantrum*, and *Limelite, Luv & Niteclubz*. Her best-known features are with Jermaine Dupri, Kris Kross, Mariah Carey, Missy Elliott, Jay-Z, Aaliyah, and the Notorious B.I.G. The smash hit "Not Tonight," with Lil' Kim, Left Eye, Missy Elliott, and Angie Martinez, was Grammy nominated and an instant urban and pop radio chart topper. She has performed and written with many artists including Tyrese, Total, Xscape, Usher, Jagged Edge, Dru Hill, Destiny's Child, Kelly Price, Brandy, Bow Wow, and Snoop Dogg.

In 2015, she made her radio debut and joined the nationally syndicated *Rickey Smiley Morning Show* as the new cohost, and in 2016 became a permanent fixture on *Dish Nation*. She has also appeared on *The Parent 'Hood*, *Sabrina the Teenage Witch*, *All That*, *Rickey Smiley for Real*, *Empire*, and *The Rap Game*, recapping every episode of the latter on a show titled *Da Brat Game*. She also selectively produced We TV's *Growing Up Hip Hop: Atlanta*.

In 2018, Da Brat made a successful live theater debut as Cleo from the hit 1996 movie *Set It Off*.

In 2021, she made television history with her partner, Jesseca Harris-Dupart, as an executive producer and cast member on We TV's *Brat Loves Judy*, which aired for three seasons, along with *Brat Loves Judy: The Baby Special*—making them the first LGBTQ+ female power couple featured on reality television. Da Brat also appeared on *Nick Cannon Presents: Wild 'n Out*, *The Wendy Williams Show*, *The Chi*, and *Queens*.

Da Brat continues to flourish in her acting and music career by writing and producing as well as developing new talent. Along with special appearances, performances, and speaking engagements, she also lends her time to charitable organizations such as Kaleidoscope Kares, Kamileon's Kloset, Hosea Feed the Hungry, and Saving Our Daughters.